Recovery from Addiction

The Way Doctors Do It

The characters in this book are not real individuals,
rather they are composites. The incidents and conversations
are recreated from memory, supplemented with the author's
experience and that of countless others.

Permission is granted to quote from this work for the purpose
of reviews and discussions.
Permission to quote from the Big Book of Alcoholics
Anonymous provided by AA World Services, Inc.
Permission to quote from the works of Dylan Thomas
provided by David Higham Associates, London.

This work was previously published as "A Spiritual
Pathway to Recovery From Addiction."

Recovery from Addiction,
The Way Doctors Do It.
© 2021 Linville M. Meadows. All rights reserved.
Published by The Meadows Farm, Inc.
Cover photographs by the Author.

ISBN eBook edition   978-1-7350258-5-8

*"I woke up on my 49th birthday and realized that I was
addicted to drugs and alcohol and that my life
was spinning wildly out of control.*

*No matter how hard I tried, I couldn't stop.
Some days I wanted passionately to quit
and some days I just didn't care.*

*I had reached a point where I could no longer use and live.
It was either quit or die, and then something happened.*

I found recovery."

Linville M. Meadows, MD

Recovery from Addiction

The Way Doctors Do It

REVIEWS

The Prairies Book Review

Meadows takes readers through step-by-step guide to understanding the disease of addiction and how to treat it. He shares the spiritual path of recovery that become central to their lives during the rehab program. He talks about addicts' belief that their addictions are, in no way, interfering with their lives. On the contrary, they believe that addiction helps make their lives easier; it makes them forget their problems, and attain a higher state of awareness.

He shares methods for spiritual growth (such as forgiveness, gratitude, acceptance, low expectorations, helping others) and ways to incorporate moral attitudes and values into one's life (establishing new priorities, forming new habits, re-people-ization). This outstanding guide with cogent insights into the nightmarish world of addiction and recovery is a must-read for anyone who thinks he has a problem with addiction.

Ralph Snyderman, MD

Chancellor Emeritus, Duke University

This inspiring publication is a fascinating and monumental exploration of a pathway for recovery from serious addiction. If there is any book you plan to read about addiction this year, it should be this one as it will be a classic for anyone wanting to understand the mind of addicted physicians (and others) and what it takes to recover.

If there is any book you plan to read about addiction this year, it should be this one as it will be a classic for anyone wanting to understand the mind of addicted physicians (and others) and what it takes to recover. This inspiring publication is a fascinating and monumental exploration of a pathway for recovery from serious addiction.

Dr. Larry Goodman, The Goodman Factor, and author of "Fridays with Goodman."

The book's value is as a contemporary guide to recovery, set in plain English, as compared to the Big Book of Alcoholics Anonymous.

In my coaching world, there are many, many, many, many people, who have not yet reached the point of incomprehensible demoralization that is active addiction, or who are in families where addiction is rampant, who will be served by this book.

Tony Equale, Author of "An Unknown God, Essays in the Pursuit of the Sacred."

This lively, entertaining narrative of one man's appropriation of the principles and practices of the AA way of life, will open any reader's eyes to that underlying spirituality. It reveals a potential for fearless joy in daily living residing in each of us regardless if it accompanies a struggle with addiction or not.

BooksCoffee (Goodreads)

Renowned Oncologist, researcher, and the author of numerous scientific articles, Meadows writes with unflinching honesty about his time as an addict and alcoholic and his subsequent recovery through an intensive rehab program aimed at physician drinkers and presents a fascinating guide to overcome addiction.

Meadows takes readers through step-by-step guide to understanding the disease of addiction and how to treat it. He shares the spiritual path of recovery that become central to their lives during the rehab program. This outstanding guide with cogent insights into the nightmarish world of addiction and recovery is a must-read for anyone who thinks he has a problem with addiction.

Lori Yerxa, Author of Pushing Through and podcast host of Author Talk

Recovery From Addiction, by Linville M. Meadows M.D., chronicles his time in a private drug rehab for medical professionals.

This captivating memoir is written in a journal style which makes the reader feel like you are reading his daily diary. His words are candid and the banter between the others at the rehab is refreshing and insightful.

Meadows tackles each topic of the recovery process, such as ego, denial and fear in a conversational style that is easy to understand and relate to. He delves deep into the psyche of an addict and the hard process of becoming and staying sober.

This book is full of hope and will help anyone struggling with addiction or just wanting to change mindsets.

Ann Harrison Author of A Journey of Faith Paperback and podcast host of Inspirational Journeys

Although this was an educational read, It was fun and each story kept me hanging on, staying up late reading. Thanks to Lin for making this educational journey an enjoyable read.

Audrey C. Holmes, D.D., M.S.

I think this book would be useful to people considering going for treatment because it gives a personal account of what it is like. The book would also be useful to friends and families of addicts, because those who go to rehab do not share much about what they experience. People who love addicted people would appreciate insight into what going through the first step of recovery is like.

Table of Contents

Getting There	1
Where to Begin	10
Addiction is a Disease	30
Alcoholic Insanity	65
Addictive Character Traits	75
Begin with Baby Steps	96
Practical Ideas	113
Moral Inventory	123
Prayer and Meditation	141
Higher Power	153
A New Way of Thinking	167
I Can Control My Thoughts	180
I'm Starting to Wake Up	188
Living by Spiritual Principles	204
A New Way of Living	218
The Fine Points	245
Annotated Bibliography	254

Getting There

*"The journey of a thousand miles
must begin with a single step."*
—*Lao Tzu*

I was sick, scared, and lost

I stood alone in the Atlanta airport, arms full of baggage, looking for the someone who was supposed to meet me, when suddenly I dropped the bags, collapsed into an empty seat, and began to cry. I never felt more alone, more vulnerable, nor more frightened. It seemed that everything I had worked for my entire adult life was being swept away. There was no one or no thing I could turn to for help.

It seemed impossible that only five days before, my nurses had intervened on me. My alcohol and drug use had gotten completely out of control and it was obvious that I was impaired. I was sure the Medical Board would show up, arrest me, and take away my medical license. Instead, they sent me to detox. However, they issued a stern warning: failure to complete an approved rehabilitation course at a center approved for physicians would result in the permanent loss of my medical license. Complete the course, usually some three or four months, and I would be welcomed back into the medical fold with open arms.

I was at the absolute low point of my life. I had no idea what had happened to me, how a drink with dinner had become two bottles of wine every night, or how an occasional party drug had become an addiction I couldn't control. No matter how hard I tried, I couldn't quit. My life was a drunken drugged-out downward spiral. I was dying and I knew it. Some days I wanted desperately to quit. Other days I just didn't care.

Almost imperceptibly, a man about my age filled the seat beside me, caught my attention, and began to speak.

"You must be Dr. Linville Meadows," he said kindly. "What do your friends call you?"

"Lin. People only call me Linville if they're mad at me."

He put his hand out. "Name's Mike. I'm your ride to rehab. C'mon. And I promise not to call you Linville, okay?" Mike was slightly balding and stocky; his handshake was strong, and his smile was genuine. He had a good bedside manner.

"Deal. What did you say your name was?" I asked, blowing my nose.

"Mike. From New Jersey. Obstetrician. Drug of choice: more."

"More?"

"More of whatever you got," he said. I managed a small laugh. He didn't look like a drug addict and I couldn't believe he was actually telling me about his addiction. There was no one back home who I could talk to about my own problems. In fact, my days were spent terrified that someone would discover my drug use, and yet, here he was, talking openly about his.

In a few minutes, we were in his little green convertible with the top down, wheeling out of the airport. The fresh breeze felt good on my face.

"Married?" asked Mike.

"Divorced."

"Do you like riddles?" Mike asked.

"Sure, riddle me, Joker," I said.

"What creature is one part wild ravaging beast, one part angel with a heart of gold, and one part suicidal maniac?"

"At the same time?"

"Could be. Could be different times, too."

"Sounds like a Greek myth."

"Nope," he said. "Try again."

"Let me think."

"Don't," he said. "You might hurt yourself.

I was completely at a loss as to the meaning of Mike's words. But at least I wasn't crying.

The back story

Mike dropped me off at the front office and shortly I found myself sitting in front of Cameron, one of the family counselors. She would conduct my intake interview.

"Tell me what brought you here," she said gently.

So, I related the last few days of the disorder that was called my life.

My nurses had finally discovered my addiction and they sent me home. I knew my life as a physician was surely over, that the Medical Board would be waiting at my office the next morning to take me away in handcuffs. My medical license was gone forever. I went home and smoked all the pot and drank all the wine I could, but nothing could wipe out the horror that filled my brain. With nothing left to live for, I took down my shotgun, loaded it, and went outside to do myself in. Fortunately, I didn't have the courage.

The next morning when I arrived at my office, I was met by Paul, a man with a strange, quixotic grin on his face. Paul was not from the Medical Board but rather from the Physicians Recovery Network, a group that worked with the Medical Board to rehabilitate doctors who had become impaired.

He asked me if I had a problem. In a moment of clarity, I simply said, Yes. Do you want to do something about it? he asked. With no idea what "something" might be, I swallowed and said, Yes.

Within minutes, I was on my way to Richmond. Within an hour, I heard the doors of the Pleasant Green Mental Health Center slam and lock shut behind me. I was in detox.

"Am I talking too fast?" I asked Cameron. I could feel the pressure of speech upon me.

"No," she said, "you're doing just fine."

I swallowed hard, took a deep breath, and began again.

My first few days in detox in Richmond were frightening. I felt terribly out of place. I was locked up with drunks dragged out from under a bush, junkies from off the streets, prostitutes in short skirts, and one little old lady dressed in white doilies, who liked to tipple sweet wine in the dark. My craving for cocaine was always at the front of my mind. All I wanted to do was go home and get stoned.

In my first group session, we sat in a circle and introduced ourselves.

"My name's Joe," said the first. "I'm an alcoholic."

"I'm Elsie," said the second. "A junkie. Crystal meth."

It was my turn. I swallowed my pride and admitted to the world what I had become.

"I...I'm an addict," I said softly.

"Now I want each of you to share your plans for when you leave detox," said the counselor.

"I'm Billy," said a young pale man who was almost blind. "I don't know how I'm gonna stay clean. There'll be at least two dope dealers sitting on my front porch when I get home."

Ethel, a large black woman, spoke next. "I'm going to a halfway house, so I don't have to turn tricks no more."

After the session, the counselor, Ralph, pulled me aside.

"You probably have no idea what's going on here, do you?" he asked.

"Not really," I said.

"Usually," he said, "a client stays here three or four days to let the poisons drain out of their body, then they head out to a halfway house or something like that. In your case, you being a doctor and all, they got something special planned for you. Only a few places in the country know how to treat guys like you—doctors on the skids. The nearest is in Atlanta and I just made your reservation. You'll be on the plane tomorrow morning. Told them I'm sending them a bat-shit crazy oncologist."

I must have looked like a deer caught in the headlights.

"You're dying and you know it," said Ralph. "If you don't go to Atlanta, not only will you lose your license, but you'll be dead in no time. And you know I'm right."

I paused for breath, but before Cameron could speak, I plunged ahead.

My last night in detox, my brain was still swimming in a sea of drugs and booze, so my thinking was not at its very best. The next morning, I was supposed to fly to Atlanta, but the craving for cocaine was still raging inside me. My mind kept telling me that if I went to rehab for three or four months, I would have no practice left to come home to. Just saying 'to hell with it' and going home and getting wasted sounded really good. My heart, on the other hand, knew that my only hope for survival was getting on that plane.

I knelt in front of my bed like when I was four years old, folded my hands and said simply, God help me. The next morning, I packed my bag, took a taxi to the airport, and got on the plane. When we were in the sky, I remembered my prayer from the night before, but in the light of day I couldn't believe the prayer had worked for me.

"So that's it," I said. The words were flying out of my mouth. "What about me? Will I ever stop craving cocaine? What's going to happen now? How long will I have to be here? I can't possibly stay more than a few weeks. My practice will be ruined. Why are you laughing at me?"

They had what I wanted

After my meeting with Cameron, I wandered around the intake area like a lost puppy dog. Across the foyer I noticed a young black woman wearing a sweatshirt with my university's logo on it, so I walked over to say hello.

"It's comforting to see our school colors represented here," I said. "Although I'm not sure if that's a good thing or not."

"Umm, yes," she said, turning around. "It's good to see a friendly face. I'm Vera. The Board says I'm an alcoholic so I guess it must be so."

"They told me they'd take away my license if I didn't finish the program here," I said. "That got my attention."

"Mine, too," said Vera. Vera was a pathologist who spent most of her day looking at slides under the microscope. She finished a year behind me in medical school, but we had never met. She stayed on at the university to do her fellowship in Pathology then joined the faculty there.

About that time, Mike showed up. Vera headed off for her intake interview with Cameron.

"You need to know that boys and girls are strictly segregated here," said Mike. "The women's apartments are at the other end of the complex from the men. He-ing and She-ing is simply not allowed."

"Sounds pretty severe," I said.

"Here," he said, handing me a loose-leaf notebook, "this is the rule book. Read it first thing. If you break the rules, they come down on you pretty hard. You have to travel in threes, to the grocery store, to get a haircut, whatever. You must attend one meeting a day, you must be in before curfew, and you can't have your car the first month you're here."

I nodded, not quite sure what I was agreeing to.

"This is the rehab center," he said, "classrooms, offices, stuff like that." He pointed to an adjacent building. "That's Building Two, where they send you when you're been a very bad boy. It's also the center's detox wing. And where the cafeteria is." He pointed to a path leading into the woods behind the buildings. "That trail leads to an apartment complex where we live. We stay two to a bedroom, four to an apartment. There are usually between a hundred and a hundred and fifty of us drunks and junkies here at one time." He grinned. "Welcome to country club rehab."

Mike helped me carry my stuff up to the apartment, then introduced me to my new roommates.

"Guys!" he yelled out. "Hey, guys, the new fish is here. Everybody come say hello to Lin."

An athletic man in a jogging outfit came from one of the bedrooms carrying a tennis racket.

"This is John," said Mike, "a man who loves his beer and has the raunchiest sense of humor you've ever heard." He was a general surgeon from Detroit.

"Go Blue!" John said, tipping his Big Blue baseball cap and twirling a tennis racket in his hand.

"Robert here," said the portly man on the couch, raising his hand in greeting. He was wearing shorts and flip-flops and eating a doughnut. Robert was a jolly, round practitioner who never seemed to take anything too seriously. "I sleep next door but I hang out here. Family Practice. Drug of choice, crack cocaine."

The last man in the room clearly resembled Dr. Martin Luther King, Jr.

"This is Reggie," said Mike. "Our preacher from Memphis. Reggie has a fondness for bourbon and the ladies in the front row. But he's a good soul, in spite of himself."

"Stow your stuff fast," said Reggie. "We're leaving for a meeting in ten minutes. Unfortunately, John's driving."

"A meeting?" I asked. "What kind of meeting?" They all laughed at me.

"Don't pay any attention to him," said Mike to my new roommates. "He's still toxic." He turned to me. "You're required to attend at least one A. A. meeting every day."

"A.A.?" I asked.

"You know," said Robert, "A. A. Alcoholics Anonymous."

They laughed again.

"I wouldn't try thinking too much for a while," said Robert, finishing his donut and licking his fingers. "Right now, you couldn't think your way out of a wet paper bag, and you'd probably hurt yourself if you tried."

"You best follow Mike around until you get your feet on the ground," said John. "Otherwise you might get lost going to the bathroom."

These guys, like me, were not exactly at the height of their careers, but they seemed happy and full of life. I wanted that so desperately I could scream.

GETTING THERE

Deep in my addiction, I was all alone in the darkness. I was without hope.

No one could possibly understand my problems.

Intervention only works when a person is ready.

Detox allows the toxins to drain from my body but doesn't treat my disease.

Hitting a bottom: It was either quit or die. This is the turning point.

A moment of clarity can be life-saving.

You will give your old lady to the dope man for a bag of dope, and you will kill him for half a bag.

The disease of addiction affects the mind, the body, and the spirit. Any successful treatment must address all three.

Enforced sobriety can make the difference between sobriety and relapse.

Where to Begin

"No step is lost upon this path,
And no dangers are found.
And even a little progress is
Freedom from fear."
—Bhagavad Gita 2:40

Am I an alcoholic? Am I an addict?

On the way to my first AA meeting, my new friends questioned my sincerity.

"Are you a real alcoholic?" asked Robert.

"I don't know, am I?" I asked.

"That's a trick question," said Mike, lighting a cigarette. "Only you can decide if you're an alcoholic. But there are clues."

"Like, do you need an eye-opener to get the day started," said John, rolling down his window and waving the smoke away.

"Can you quit for any amount of time without going nuts?" asked Mike. He frowned and tossed his cigarette out the window. "Can you go into a bar and have two drinks and quit for the night? Can you go for six months without taking a single drink?"

I'd never thought about it like that. I was getting confused.

"It doesn't matter if you only drink after work or only on weekends," said Robert. "And it doesn't matter how much you drink. All that matters is whether you've crossed the invisible line that leads to the disease of addiction."

"Huh?" I said. They were going a little too fast for my aching brain.

"When you pass the point where you can't control your drinking anymore," said John.

"Are you having negative consequences because of your drinking?" asked Mike.

"Every time I got high, I didn't get into trouble, but every time I got into trouble, I was high," said John, looking pleased with himself.

"Are negative consequences of your drinking and drugging starting to pile up?" said Robert, "like DUIs, getting fired, having the wife and kids move out, getting hauled into court. Stuff like that."

Mike turned and stared hard at me. "Is your life ruled by your using? Will you do anything to get your drug of choice?"

That sounded like my life, sure enough.

I know the way out

We arrived at the meeting house and went in. I don't remember a thing about my first meeting.

Afterward, my jolly friend Robert came up from behind and slapped me on the back, almost bowling me over. I spilled the last of my coffee.

"What's up, dude," he bellowed. "Hey, I got a story for you. Ready?"

I wasn't sure if it mattered, but I said, "Okay. Shoot."

Robert began.

An alcoholic was stumbling down a dark city street one rainy night when he fell into a large construction pit. The sides were muddy and slicked by the rain and he couldn't get out. He began to shout.

"Help! I'm stuck in a hole and I can't get out."

Shortly, a physician walked by and hearing our drunken friend looked down into the pit.

"O my good man," said the doctor. "I can see you've fallen into a hole and can't get out. I'm a Harvard physician, don't you know, and I have something that might help." With that, the physician pulled a prescription pad from his coat, dashed off a prescription, and tossed it into the pit. "Take two of these," he said, "and call me in the morning." And he was gone.

"Merde," said the drunk, whose mother was French. He stuffed the prescription into his pocket. Shortly a preacher happened along.

"O my good man," said the preacher. "I see you've fallen in a hole and can't get out. I'm a Seminary man, don't you know, Princeton. Here, this may help." He took out a small Bible, ripped out two pages from the Psalms, and threw them into the pit. "Read two of these and call me in the morning," he said. And he was gone.

"Sheist," said the drunk, whose father was German. He now doubted if any help was possible, but just then a strange man with a broad smile peered into the pit.

"Help!" cried our friend. "I had too much to drink and fell into this hole and can't get out. The doctor gave me a prescription and the preacher gave me a Psalm, but I'm still in the pit."

"Don't worry, my friend," said the man. "I know what to do."

With that, the stranger leapt into the pit with the drunk.

"Oh, no!' cried the drunk. "Now we're both stuck in here. That was a pretty stupid thing to do."

"Not at all,' said our rescuer. "I'm a recovering alcoholic. I've been here before and I know the way out."

I laughed. "I hope you know the way out."

"No," said Robert, "but I know where the all-night cafe is. Wanna get something to eat?"

You don't have to do it anymore

The next morning, as Mike and I walked the path through the woods to the treatment center, the sky was overcast and gray. It seemed as if a thousand-pound weight was hung around my neck. Just looking up hurt my eyes. Mike took pity on me.

"Did somebody run over your puppy dog this morning?" he asked.

I mumbled a response but didn't feel like talking.

"I guess this is probably the low point in your miserable life," he said.

I glared but did not speak.

"Drugs of choice: cocaine and alcohol, I'll bet."

I glared louder.

"There is one good thing about all this."

"What?" I barked.

"You don't have to do it anymore."

Setting out

I was sitting in Cameron's group for newcomers. More than anything, I was glad to be out of the chaotic hateful world that had been my life. No one was supposed to know where I was, and the center was not allowed to acknowledge that I was here. If I was isolated from the world of my old life, at least I wasn't in the middle of it anymore.

"Setting out on a long journey can take a lot of preparation," said Cameron. "I may need to find a house sitter, stop the newspaper, put the cat in a kennel, order tickets, make reservations, and so on. The spiritual trip you're beginning will occupy the rest of your life, so a lot of getting ready will be necessary. For some of you, the difficulties involved will cause you to quit. That's cool. You can always come back later if you want to. But for those of you who succeed, the difficulties of the path must be balanced by the depth of the commitment you make at the start," she said, opening a book.

"When the world has beaten you over the head for so long that your eyes are filled with blood, when your chest is so heavy you can't breathe, and when your children won't return your phone calls, it's hard to believe that human beings are essentially good. When your best drinking buddy steals your wallet, your girl, and your stash, forgiveness won't be your first thought. When the IRS is knocking on your door, the power company has cut off your lights, and the checks you bounced have come home to roost, it's hard to find joy in the morning. And when all the lies, deceit, and pain you have caused others becomes a burden you can no longer carry, it's time for a change." She paused and looked up. I, of course, was sure she was talking to me. She continued.

"The image of essential goodness, based on that tiniest piece of divinity burning inside each of us, is a powerful idea. To move from hopeless to hope, I had to grasp the idea that I was a good person. That I was basically honest, no matter how many lies I had told. That I was kind, no matter how many people I had hurt. That I was capable of change, no matter how many times I had failed. Finding hope in the midst of my ruined, burned-out world was absolutely essential. I had to learn that I was worthy of love."

"Hearing the stories of other alcoholics gave me reason to trust. When I heard my story come from their lips, I knew I wasn't alone. We had shared the same experiences. They understood. Our position in society, the size of our fathers' checkbooks, or the cars we drive are insignificant compared with our common dilemma."

"Somehow tied up in all this was the idea that we are all children of God. I took hold of this notion without much understanding of what it meant, for it filled some hole in my heart that needed filling. If we were all children of God, then we all had value, even the worst drunks and junkies of the world. If I was a child of God, my nature was good and only my behavior was bad. If I were a bad person, there would be no help for me, but if I were a good person with bad behavior then my behavior could be changed." She put the book down.

"One of our former clients wrote that."

My roommate John was speaking at our house check-in group one afternoon. For once, he had left his tennis racket behind.

"Yeah," he said, "I lived under a black cloud. My sole purpose on any given day was to consume enough beer to numb myself."

"What happened?" I asked. "Short version."

"A friend took me to an A. A. meeting. Made me pick up a white chip," he said. "At the time I thought it was stupid, but it started me thinking. I couldn't conceive of never drinking for the rest of my life. That just wasn't possible. But maybe I could do it for just one day—today—then come back tomorrow. That was all they asked. Just one day."

Robert spoke up. "My psychiatrist told me that I had used up a lifetime supply of drugs and alcohol. The cupboard was bare, she said. Somehow, that seemed to make a lot of sense."

Everything you think you know is wrong

Mike would become my mentor in recovery. He repeatedly pointed me in the right direction whenever I wandered off the path. One afternoon, we were sitting in the breezeway outside the apartment, drinking coffee while he smoked a cigarette.

"You're not going to like this," he said, "but everything you think you know is wrong." Then he waited for me to deny it. I didn't disappoint him.

"Hold on there!" I said. "I made Dean's List, graduated with Honors, and…"

"And, all that fine knowledge of yours landed you here in rehab," he said, "now didn't it?"

I knew he was right, but I wasn't going down without a fight. My ego wouldn't let me.

"Yes, but…" I blustered.

"I'm not talking about how to change a tire or drive from here to Richmond," he said. "I'm talking about how to behave in the world, how to feel good about yourself, and how to live a life where anger isn't your primary emotion."

I was squirming in my seat, but I sipped my coffee and listened.
"When I got here, I was sure I knew it all—who I was, what my problem was, and what I needed to do about it," he said. "Then Cameron told me what I just told you."

"Everything you think I know is wrong?" I asked.

"Yup," he said. "And it was as big a shock to me then as it is to you now. And just like you, I refused to believe it."

The late spring breeze cooled my aching head. I went inside and refilled my coffee then rejoined Mike outside.

"As my head cleared, I began to see how screwed up my thinking had become," he said. "The deterioration was so slow that I never realized it was happening. Cameron said that I didn't need to fix just one or two things, I needed a whole new way of looking at the world, a whole new way of thinking." That sounded like way too much for me to handle all at once. It must have shown on my face, for Mike said, "Baby steps, my friend, baby steps. And remember—it was your very best thinking that got you here."

Morning spiritual

"First stop of the day, morning spiritual," said Robert, finishing off a Danish as we walked through the woods to Building Two. "Promptly at 8:45, we assemble for a short spiritual lesson to start the day off right."

"You got to be kidding," I said. "I gave up on that stuff a long time ago."

"Look, doofus," he said with an edge to his voice. "If you knew all the answers, you goddamn wouldn't be here. Everything you think you know is wrong. And I mean everything."

Mike's words from the day before echoed in my head.

"Consider, if you will," he said, calming down, "that maybe you threw the baby out with the bathwater."

We walked silently into a large room and were greeted by Father Mick, a tall geeky man dressed in a soutane. He handed a stack of pages to John, who distributed them around the room. On each was the 38th Psalm.

"Father Mick is our spiritual advisor," said Mike, standing beside me. "He's been sober four years and worked here most of that time. Really cool dude."

I nodded, lest my words get me in trouble again.

"I suspect," said Father Mick from the podium, once the room became quiet, "that addiction has always been with us. Every time I read this Psalm, it reminds me of how I felt at the end of my drinking career. Maybe you can hear your story in it as well. The verse does end on a positive note, that there is hope for even the worst of us. And, of course, my enemies are the negative thoughts in my mind."

He began to read.

"O LORD, rebuke me not in thy wrath: neither chasten me in thy hot displeasure. For thine arrows stick fast in me, and thy hand presseth me sore. There is no soundness in my flesh because of thine anger; neither is there any rest in my bones because of my sin. For mine iniquities are gone over mine head: as a heavy burden they are too heavy for me.

My wounds stink and are corrupt because of my foolishness. I am troubled; I am bowed down greatly; I go mourning all the day long. For my loins are filled with a loathsome disease: and there is no soundness in my flesh. I am feeble and sore broken: I have roared by reason of the disquietness of my heart.

Lord, all my desire is before thee; and my groaning is not hid from thee. My heart panteth, my strength faileth me: as for the light of mine eyes, it also is gone from me.

My lovers and my friends stand aloof from my sore; and my kinsmen stand afar off. They also that seek after my life lay snares for me: and they that seek my hurt speak mischievous things, and imagine deceits all the day long.

But I, as a deaf man, heard not; and I was as a dumb man that openeth not his mouth. Thus, I was as a man that heareth not, and in whose mouth are no reproofs.

For in thee, O LORD, do I hope: thou wilt hear, O Lord my God. For I said, Hear me, lest otherwise they should rejoice over me: when my foot slippeth, they magnify themselves against me. For I am ready to halt, and my sorrow is continually before me.

For I will declare mine iniquity; I will be sorry for my sin. But mine enemies are lively, and they are strong: and they that hate me wrongfully are multiplied. They also that render evil for good are mine adversaries; because I follow the thing that good is.

Forsake me not, O LORD: O my God, be not far from me. Make haste to help me, O Lord my salvation."

Father Mick looked up and smiled.

I felt vaguely comforted by the words, but I couldn't see how that had anything to do with me.

On the way to my newcomer session, I suddenly felt the uncontrollable urge to get high, rolling over me like a wave, frightening in its strength. The imaginary rush of the drug hitting my bloodstream moved over me like so many times before. Like before, the craving took control of my entire being. I felt the inside of my arm where the needle had lived, and rubbed the tired weary veins. I looked around nervously to see if anyone had noticed my slide back down the rabbit hole. Afraid of swooning, I leaned back against the wall and closed my eyes. Then, I felt someone touch my arm, and opened my eyes to find Mike standing by my side. He knew.

"C'mon friend," he said kindly. "We gotta get you out a here. Let's go find some coffee."

His touch broke the spell and snapped me back to reality, but the memory lingered all day, and I kept looking warily over my shoulder for its return.

We were sitting around after dinner when John, leaning against the door frame, tennis racket in hand, told this story.

"I was blind drunk when I left home," he said, "but I didn't think anything was wrong with my driving."

We laughed at that.

"Within minutes, I was craving another beer," he said, "so I stopped at a mini-mart and bought a six-pack. I drank most of the beer in the parking lot, then wheeled onto the road in my best imitation of Richard Petty, when I saw the flashing red and blue lights behind me. The policeman politely asked me if I was having a problem."

"I just nodded my head, knowing I'd slur my words. The officer clearly saw the empty beer cans on the floor, but for some reason he took pity on me, knowing I would never pass a breathalyzer test.

"'Okay,' he said. 'If you promise to go straight home and not stop on the way, I'll let you go this one time.'"

"I think they call that enabling," said Mike in a hushed voice.

John continued. "I drank the last two beers on the side of the road and then my craving returned. I drove two blocks to the next mini-mart and bought another six-pack. Within minutes, the flashing lights were again in my rear-view mirror. A different officer not only gave me a DUI, but he handcuffed me and hauled me off to jail.

"You know, the whole time, I couldn't understand why the police were hassling me. I was a careful, safe driver, I thought. I was sure my thinking and my reflexes were completely normal."

"That sounds terribly insane," I said.

"I've thought the same thing myself," said John, tossing his tennis racket into the air and catching it.

"I think you may be an alcoholic," said Mike.

Take the cotton out of your ears and put it in your mouth

We were at a Friday night A. A. meeting near the university. It was a speaker meeting, where one person tells the story of their addiction and how they recovered. Tonight, the speaker was Frank, an insurance salesman. He was tall, thin, and a little mousy. I kept thinking; would I buy insurance from this man?

"Early in my sobriety," he began, "I was sure I knew everything, so there was no need for me to listen to you. In fact, I was sure you wanted me to point out all of your faults and tell you how to fix them."

The crowd laughed and somber Frank smiled, just a little.

"This old way of thinking had become so ingrained that I resisted any new ideas, especially if they came from you. Today, I know that I am an egomaniac with an inferiority complex. But in those days, to hide my low self-esteem, I had to be smarter than you. I had to be right all the time. Especially at A. A. and N.A. meetings."

Another round of laughter. Frank's smile grew a little bigger.

"Today, when I see newcomers arrive in the rooms with this same attitude, I marvel at what an arrogant asshole I was then. That's not to say that I'm not an arrogant asshole now, because I am. But today, I can listen and learn, and I know that while my experience can help others, my advice is worth nothing." He paused for a sip of coffee.

Mike giggled. In my ear he whispered, "Kinda sounds like you, don't it?"

"Someone told me," Frank continued, "to take the cotton out of my ears and put it in my mouth. Meaning of course that when I'm talking, I can't hear what you're saying. Remember, recovery is all about turning our lives around, so it's important to hear what others with more clean and sober time have to say."

Frank wiped his brow and smiled out loud.

Mike punched me in the ribs and giggled again. My face was hot with embarrassment. Frank's words rang true for me, but I was frightened because I had never questioned my intellect so deeply.

Stinking thinking

The next morning, I was introduced to Matt's group session. Matt was about my age but far thinner and more athletic. He had short-cropped hair and a short beard that was salt and pepper gray. The story was that Matt had been chaplain to the Special Forces at Fort Campbell before he came to Taylor. They also said he was an ordained Catholic priest, but then they said a lot of things. I settled into a seat at the back of the room and tried to keep my head down.

"Welcome to the school for impaired physicians," Matt said. "I hope you enjoy your stay with us here at the asylum."

That brought more than a few puzzled looks from his audience.

"Didn't they tell you; this place is a state-licensed mental hospital? If you don't believe me, look on the sign on the back of the front door where you come in."

"You are, of course, all mentally compromised beyond your understanding," he said. "How is that, you say? Well, to discuss all the forms of alcoholic insanity would require more time than we have today. So, let's concentrate on your stinking thinking."

"What?" I blurted out, then instantly regretted it.

"Who are you?" Matt looked me straight in the eye.

"Lin," I whispered.

"Yeah, I've heard about you," he said. "The crazy cancer doctor from Virginia. Got it," he nodded at me. "Do you know what stinking thinking is?"

"Uh, no," I said.

"Well, you've got it in spades," he laughed. "In fact, your thinking smells so bad you're stinking up the whole room." The group laughed, glad it wasn't them getting roasted. "Robert, can you help us out here?"

Robert sucked air for a moment, then said, "There are at least three ways Lin's thinking is screwed up. He has a damaged thinker, a broken filter, and an overactive forgetter."

"And why is your thinker broken, Lin?" asked Matt.

"Because I used a lot of coke and drank a lot of wine?" I squeaked.

"Good," said Matt. "Maybe there's hope for you after all. And what about your broken filter, Mike?"

"A normal brain filters out all the useless input it gets," said Mike. "You know, highway noise, flashing neon signs, background conversation in a restaurant. My filter has been refitted to help me stay drunk. Anything which suggests that my using is causing a problem is filtered out. Nothing critical of my using behavior gets in."

"Your broken filter screens out all the warnings from your friends, ignores the damage that you're doing to your body, and everything your conscience is trying to tell you," said Matt. "John?"

"Just in case anything gets by my filter," John said, "I've developed an overactive forgetter. I can instantly forget anything which might compromise my drinking and drugging. I can ignore the warning the cop just gave me. I can forget my wife telling me that if I don't quit drinking, she'd leave me. I can forget the bank threatening to repossess my car. I can forget anything which threatens to interfere with my using. It's all very convenient."

"But I don't understand," I peeped.

Matt turned and stared straight at me. "Lin, my friend," he said, "you are sicker than you know."

I gulped. I was standing at the edge of a precipice with no bottom in sight. I could no longer trust my best friend, my wonderful brain, and I was frightened.

Trustworthy

The next day, Matt was nailing a newcomer's butt to the wall.

"Chuck," Matt began, "Are you trustworthy?"

"Of course," stuttered Chuck. "I'm as honest as the next guy."

"That's not what I asked." Matt turned and looked at Mike. "Mike, what did I ask?"

"You asked Chuck if he was trustworthy."

Matt looked at Robert and asked, "You've never met Chuck, have you??" Robert shook his head. "Is he trustworthy?"

"Absolutely not, sir," Robert said. "Chuck's an untreated alcoholic. He's neither trustworthy nor honest."

Chuck was red-faced and squirming.

"Vera, of all the people in this room, who does Chuck trust?"

"No one," said Vera. "He's not capable of trust."

"What will happen if Chuck doesn't learn how to trust?"

"His ship will sail over the edge of the world and he'll die!" she said sweetly.

Matt looked sadly at Chuck. "Failure to trust breeds dishonesty," he said. "If I can't trust you with who I am, I can't share my true feelings with you. My secret self, afraid of being hurt, will hide every vulnerability. To become trustworthy, you must first learn to trust yourself. Then, and only then, can you begin to trust others."

As we walked back to the apartments, Robert was thoughtful.

"I remember when I first started to trust," he said. "For the three days I spent in detox in Miami, I was too sick to hear anything. When I got here, Terry, he was here before you, took me under his wing and led me around by the nose. Took me to my first A. A. meeting. Up to that point, I was afflicted by what they call terminal uniqueness. That is, nobody had ever been through the stuff I had, and no one could possibly understand me, or my problems. Which is, of course, just denial on my part. See, if I'm unique then I don't have to listen to you and I can keep on using, and probably dying, which is why they call it terminal uniqueness."

I nodded, barely avoiding tripping over a tree root in the path.

"Anyway, at the meeting one night, this old guy was telling his story," said Robert. "He looked like a street bum, all bent over, shabby clothes, nothing like me at all. I thought, what could I possibly have in common with this guy? But as he talked, it was as if he was telling my story. If I had written it down and had him read it, it couldn't have been more like my life. We had done the same drug, fought the same battles, and been beaten down together."

We emerged from the woods and headed across the parking lot toward our apartment. The sky was overcast and angry and threatened a pure Georgia thunderstorm. We hurried along as only two chubby doctors can. In the apartment, Robert pulled out a Little Debbie cake from the pantry and plopped down on the couch. I put on the coffee as Robert continued his tale.

"It was amazing," he said. "This guy understood what I'd been through. I wasn't alone anymore." He munched and recollected. "So, I felt I could trust him. Then I looked at Terry, and I knew I could trust him, too."

I poured us coffee and sat down.

"These guys, they were just like me, and maybe, just maybe, what they were saying was true. I had a glimmer of hope that maybe I could get this monkey off my back."

He polished off the last of little Debbie, licked his fingers, and asked plaintively, "Who's cooking tonight?"

Timmy

Timmy arrived at rehab with his mouth shut. A pharmacist from the Midwest, he was thin and blond, and I was sure that a strong breeze would blow him over.

"I think he expects to get out of here without saying anything," said Robert as we headed out to the evening's A. A. meeting.

"Good luck with that," I said.

"I asked him to come over tonight so we could talk," said Robert.

Timmy dutifully arrived at the apartment about 9:30, and as usual, John put on another pot of coffee. We filled our cups. Timmy, true to form, sat quietly, his face a picture of sorrow.

"So, you're from Dubuque?" I asked.

"Des Moines," said Timmy, trying to smile. "Dubuque is about 200 miles east of Des Moines."

"It's all the Great Plains to me," I said, trying to be funny.

"I heard your thing was speed," said John.

"Well, uh, yeah," said Timmy. "I used to go back to the pharmacy at night to do paperwork, but instead I'd grind up Ritalin and inject myself. I eventually reached a point where I would inject myself in the morning on the way to work. No matter how upset or sad I was, Ritalin always took away my problems."

"Speed can do that," I agreed, "at least for a while."

"So I found out," said Timmy.

"What's your sex thing?" asked Robert, who was sprawled out on the couch making love to a slice of left-over pizza. One of Robert's pet theories was that everybody in rehab had a sex thing, so he always asked. The new fish always denied it, but within a few weeks you would hear them would brag about spending $3,000 in one night at a strip bar, or something similar.

"Me?" said Timmy, acting surprised. "I don't have a sex thing!"

This brought a round of applause from the group. Timmy sank perceptibly deeper into his sadness.

"I hear you play the guitar," I said, for I had seen him unload a guitar case with his suitcases. I noticed because I play as well. Everyone had gone to bed by the time Timmy returned with his guitar. I had trouble keeping my eyes open, but I tuned my guitar and tried to forget about getting up in the morning. We played together for over an hour until Timmy stopped in mid-song and began to cry.

"Robert was right," he said. "I was having an affair with one of the salesgirls at the pharmacy. We'd meet behind the counter after lights out and play doctor. Then Alice—that's my wife—found out, and my world began to unravel." He wiped a sleeve across his face. "I'm going to lose the pharmacy, my license, and my family. My life is over—I've screwed up beyond any possible repair."

"Maybe it's not all that bad," I said, laying my guitar aside. I stood up and gave him a hug. He started crying again.

We will love you until you learn to love yourself

John was on my ass. I wasn't feeling very good about myself. Depressed, my career in shambles, I felt hopelessly alone. John could see it on my face. He pointed his tennis racket at me and began to rant.

"In group today, didn't you hear Matt say, 'We'll love you until you learn to love yourself?' Does that make any sense to you at all, you numb-skull?"

"Not really," I said. "I haven't loved myself in a very long time. I've made so many mistakes and hurt so many people, I don't see how anybody could love me."

"We all felt that way when we got here," said Robert.

"And...?" I asked.

"We let them love us," Robert said.

That sounded like bullshit from a sappy greeting card, and I said so.

"We're all children of God," said Reggie the preacher, who was sitting by the window, watching the rain fall outside. He turned to face me and said, "Within each of us is a small piece of goodness, a little bit of divinity." He got up and walked across the room to sit down beside me. "It's where your conscience is. It's how you know right from wrong. It's where love comes from."

"I'm not sure I know how to love," I said. "There's just this big empty hole where my heart used to be."

"Doofus!" John was waving his tennis racket again. "Didn't I just tell you; we'll love you til you learn how to love yourself?" His love was shouting at me.

I looked at Reggie. "What's he talking about?" I asked.

"What John means is that every newcomer feels just like you do now. All of us did. Unloved, lonely, afraid."

I nodded. That sounded like me.

"In time, we came to understand that we have a bad disease but we're good people at heart. That as children of God, the real part of us is good, kind, honest, and worthy. Loveable, in spite the wrongs we'd done," he said. "Recovery can be thought of as controlling our disease and letting that essential goodness out."

In a moment of silence, we all stared out the window at the rain, calming and peaceful.

"We're all worthy of love," said Reggie softly. "The more I can love others, the more I can love myself."

Where To Begin

Only I can decide if I am an alcoholic or an addict.

Am I having negative consequences from my using?

Except in rare circumstances, I need a guide to show me the pathway to recovery.

Hearing the stories of other addicts helped me to begin to trust again.

They told me I was a child of God, and that struck a chord deep inside.

I am a good person with a bad disease.

Finding long-term recovery requires a complete rearrangement of my mind and spirit.

Everything I think I know is wrong for my mind has been warped by my addiction.

I must learn to listen to the wisdom of others.

The love of those who are ahead of me on the path to recovery is essential for me to love myself.

Addiction is a Disease

*"I hold a beast, an angel and a madman in me,
and my enquiry is as to their working,
and my problem is their subjugation and victory,
downthrow and upheaval,
and my effort is their self-expression."*
—Dylan Thomas

The Beast, the Angel, and the Madman

Cameron was leading the group. She was the favorite among the guys, for she was the youngest staffer by ten years. She was a pretty brunette with a pageboy haircut that only a slim woman can pull off. I was falling in love with her.

"I'm sure most of you are familiar with Dylan Thomas, the Welsh poet," she began. "Not only was he famous for his beautiful poems, but he was possibly the worst drunkard ever to pick up a pen. He died of chronic alcoholism at the age of 39."

"He did have a remarkable insight into his illness and described it as having three parts: the beast, the angel, and the madman. I quote, 'I hold a beast, an angel and a madman in me, and my enquiry is as to their working, my problem is their subjugation and victory, downthrow and upheaval, and my effort is their self-expression.' This is a good place to begin our inquiry into the nature of the disease of alcoholism, of addiction. Thomas once told a friend—admittedly while intoxicated—that he drank to reconcile the disorder outside and the order within himself. Sound familiar to anyone?"

A murmur spread through the room.

"The beast: in each of us, Thomas suggests, lives a beast that is capable of anything—absolutely anything—from simply wreaking havoc in the lives of others to committing murder. Like Dr. Jekyll's Mr. Hyde, the beast is completely without morals of any kind and lives only to destroy. There are those who would deny that such a monster lives within them. 'Oh, I would never do that,' they say, referring to the terrors committed by their fellow man, but they simply don't know what they are truly capable of. The horrible truth is, under the right circumstances, like being stoked up on crack cocaine, our murderous Mr. Hyde will come screaming out."

I knew about Hyde.

Cameron continued, "The madman: at the core of our addiction lies a peculiar insanity. Certainly, we've pickled our brains with all the poisons we used, but most of those effects will fade with time. However, the insanity of our addiction appears to be hard-wired in. No matter how long we have been sober nor how spiritually fit we may appear to be, lurking somewhere in our subconscious is the notion that one day we can drink again like other people. At some weak moment, some stressed-out afternoon when we least expect it, the sudden uncontrollable urge to drink and use will rise again to threaten us. Without some recourse to a power greater than ourselves, we will drink again."

"The angel: a number of us have considered a life in religion, though usually with little success," said Cameron. "My sponsor was kicked out of divinity school for playing piano at music bars. My evangelist grandfather kept a still behind the barn. Those of us who didn't seek a religious life at least thought about it. Strange as it may sound, in us drunks and junkies there exists a strong and unquenchable spiritual thirst. This spirituality underlies our hunger for meaning and our search for an explanation for existence. This yearning holds the key to our recovery. This is our saving grace, our Angel."

I wasn't sure if an angel had ever touched my life. Hunger for meaning? Certainly.

"During your time here, you'll learn about the nature of your disease and how it can be treated. But most of all, you'll learn about yourselves."

The men in the room all applauded.

She also said that we were sicker than we knew, but it would be months before I could understand the truth of that. I only knew one thing, that I was scared to death, the most frightened I had ever been in my life. For my own Mr. Hyde, a monster of unimaginable horror, had sprung forth from within me and I would do anything—absolutely anything—to keep that creature from ever appearing again.

The disease concept

"May I ask a stupid question?" I asked as we walked to the center.

"I didn't know you could ask any other kind," said Robert, huffing and puffing along the trail.

"Go ahead," said Mike, trying to smoke and walk at the same time.

"What is addiction, anyway?" I asked. "I mean, I thought I knew, but now I'm not so sure. Nobody here looks like a rummy in the gutter or a wino panhandling on a corner."

"Ah, the first sign of progress," said John, sprinting effortlessly up from behind. "The good doctor admits he doesn't know. There may be hope for you yet, my boy."

"Don't be so hard on him," said Robert. "He's just a newcomer. Only an egg."

We paused for breath, the summer morning muggy and warm.

"Let me help you out here," said Mike. "Addiction's an illness, just like diabetes or any other chronic disease."

"Lots of people think it's a moral weakness," said Robert. "The drunkard stumbling on the street has succumbed to the temptations of the Devil and Demon Rum."

"They can't understand why I don't just quit, like they did," said John. "Those without the disease—we call them Earth People—have little hope of ever understanding it."

Shortly, we were in the main building and headed for the lounge.

"Which is why we have to stick together," said Reggie, who joined us at the communal coffeepot. "We're a fellowship of the most unlikely companions."

"The disease concept is important," said Robert, "because if I'm a bad person, there's no hope for me. I'll just go on being bad forever. But if I'm a good person with a bad disease, I can treat my illness and find a good life."

"I'm a good person with a bad disease," I repeated.

"You have a chronic, relapsing, and fatal disease," said Mike.

"But it can be treated, right?" I asked.

"Certainly," said Robert. "Now let give you the best definition of addiction I've ever heard. It came from a young man named Phillip."

A feeling disease

It was a nasty moonless night, shaken by a hellish Georgia lightning storm when the police delivered Phillip to detox, half-naked, barefoot and in handcuffs, out of his mind, drenched. Phillip was a young, well-muscled black man, tall and angry, very angry. He had gone soldiering in the Middle East for his country and returned with a purple heart and a monkey on his back. He lived on the street, psychotic, and shooting heroin.

On his first day in detox, Phillip covered his head with a blanket and refused to speak. No one dared speak to him. The second day, he pulled the blanket over his shoulders like an Indian brave and glared at everyone in the room. Still, no one would speak to Phillip. The third day, he raised his hand (his medicines were beginning to kick in) and gave the best definition for addiction I've ever heard.

"My name is Phillip," he said gently, "and I have a feeling disease. I will do anything I can to change the way I feel."

We were standing around the auditorium waiting for Dr. Taylor to arrive. Taylor, an alcoholic himself, had founded the rehab center specifically for the treatment of the impaired physician.

"I didn't drink for the taste," said John, "I drank for the effect."

"I don't understand," I said. I seemed to be saying that a lot lately.

"Understanding is highly overrated," he said, "but in my confused state, those kind words were not terribly helpful.

"I hated the taste of beer, but it got me drunk and then I didn't care anymore. Dull, boring John became the life of the party. I could flirt with the girls. Leap tall buildings at a single bound. I was King of the World." He held his coffee cup high. "When I got drunk, I no longer felt that horribly uncomfortable feeling most people call life. In time, I switched from beer to vodka. It worked faster."

"There are a thousand things I can do to change the way I feel," said Reggie, "and if I can do it more than once, I can become addicted to it. And almost anything can change the way I feel. Reminds me of my roommate freshman year in college. I'm pretty sure he was an alcoholic. He always had a beer in his hand and I never did see him crack a book."

"Not useful for success at the university," said Mike.

"His parents were well-to-do," Reggie said. "He drove a new BMW. Every time he flunked a test and felt bad, he'd go into town and buy new clothes. He was sort of a clothes horse anyway. Always looked real spiffy."

"Changed the way he felt, I suspect," said Mike.

"I'm sure," Reggie said. "I wasn't surprised when he flunked out after the first semester."

Mike grinned, "Yeah, but I'll bet he had a great wardrobe."

Dr. Taylor arrived and we took our seats.

"Back in the '60s," Dr. Taylor began, "I toured the Bowery to see what the most famous drunks in the world were like. There I met another physician who had lost his way. He panhandled on the street to buy wine and lived in an empty tenement with no utilities but no rent. Together, we discussed the nature of our illness. Then, to my surprise, he pulled out a needle and injected himself with a large dose of magnesium sulfate."

Mike leaned over and whispered, "Epsom salts." He laughed.

Taylor continued, "Then he went over behind a post and had an enormous bowel movement. I asked him what in the hell he was doing. He said, 'Well, it's the least expensive way to change the way I feel. Cheaper than heroin.'"

"We're a strange lot," quipped Mike.

I had to nod, barely able to believe what I was hearing.

One disease

After the necessary coffee and cigarette break on the patio, we headed to Matt's classroom.

"Welcome to drunk and junkie school," said Matt, as I took my seat. I saw Vera in the back and waved but said nothing.

"You'll find that all the seats in this room are the same, regardless of who you think you are," said Matt. "No matter what you used to believe, today you'll learn that you all share the same disease, the disease of addiction. In this room, a drunk is the same as a junkie and an alcoholic is the same as an addict. There's no difference between a judge who tipples too much and is escorted home by a deputy sheriff, and the junkie sleeping in the street who's arrested by the same deputy. The nurse who steals pain pills from her patients' medicine drawer is no different than the addicted housewife in the ER, dying of an overdose of opioids."

"The image most of us have of the alcoholic is a wizened old man panhandling for spare change and living under a bridge," he said. "Our picture of the addict is a skanky prostitute living in an abandoned building who turns just enough tricks to shoot up again. But this isn't the true face of addiction. Over seventy percent of us lead relatively normal lives. We go to work, pay at least some of our bills, and maintain a semblance of a loving family life. We're still functional, although our lives are usually far from happy and probably unmanageable. Just because you still have a job making good money doesn't mean you're not one of us."

"It's not for me or anyone else to say whether you are an addict or an alcoholic. Only you can decide if your drinking and using have gotten out of control. Hearing that you are a drunk from your wife, your boss, your doctor, or your judge isn't helpful. What you used isn't important either: beer is the same as wine or bourbon and they're the same as pot, or crack, or meth. And it doesn't matter how much you drink or use. All that matters is whether you have crossed over that invisible line that separates heavy using from true addiction."

Sitting in the back of the room, I suddenly realized that my palms were sweaty and I was scared shitless.

Quit or die

Mike and I were sitting in the cafeteria after everyone else had left. I added sugar to the dregs of my coffee and stirred.

"Well," asked Mike, "When did you realize that it was either quit or die?"

I didn't have to think long before I answered. "I was sitting home one evening, wasted as usual, watching the sunset through the picture window of my new and very expensive house, when I realized that I'd never be able to quit using my precious cocaine. I knew with absolute certainty that one day I would die chasing the dope dealer down a dark alleyway."

I looked up into my roommate's face and could feel my tears welling up.

"It was hopeless. I didn't care about anything. Not my career, not my family, nothing. Certainly not myself. I would have committed suicide but I'm too much of a coward. I had reached some dark acceptance that I was going to die, but you know what, I just didn't give a damn. I just wanted it all to be over."

We sat in silence for a while.

"Fortunately, at that point, they intervened on me," I said.

During Matt's session, Ryan, recently arrived in rehab, stood up and read a poem he had written. He was a neurologist and literally tall, dark, and handsome. His poem was about a flower that lived in his hometown in Hawaii. As he spoke, he seemed too sensitive for the manly body he inhabited. His girlfriend was incredibly beautiful and had flown all the way from Honolulu just to be with him. Ryan seemed to have everything going his way—good looks, great job making tons of money, living in paradise, and dating a beautiful woman, except for the fact that he was a heroin addict and he couldn't quit.

We spoke afterward. I was impressed by his gentleness. And he was frighteningly candid.

"I can't do it, Lin," he said. "I can't walk across that bed of coals." He looked down sadly as if a giant pit of fiery orange flames was staring back at him, forbidding him to cross over into recovery. He shook his head and walked away.

He left rehab a few days later without saying a word to anyone. He hadn't completed his treatment. He just up and left.

About two weeks later, Mike caught me in the hall.

"You remember, Ryan, the guy who read that sappy poem?" he asked.

"Yeah," I remembered. "The guy who had everything to live for."

"Well," Mike said sadly. "He's dead. Died of a heroin overdose back in Hawaii."

My face fell. Ryan had reached the point of quit or die. But overcoming his addiction was simply beyond his reach. The pain of living was no longer bearable but he couldn't summon the courage to cross his personal bed of coals. Dying was the only answer left. For Ryan, it took the form of a syringe full of heroin.

Powerlessness

Dr. Taylor called a special afternoon session to discuss the concept of powerlessness. Someone had complained that the current crop of clients was having trouble wrapping their heads around this central idea.

"I remember when I first recognized my own powerlessness," he began. "I was so deep in denial, I couldn't see that my disease had taken complete control of my life. I began each day with an eye-opener. Lunch was always a two-martini affair. I would leave the office early to be home before the sun was over the yardarm. Wine with dinner became good social graces, and I single-handedly invented the custom of the double nightcap. Yet I didn't have a drinking problem, not even when I was flagged for three DUIs inside a month, and the judge, my good golfing buddy, took away my driver's license. They were the ones with the problem, not me!"

"Only when I began to have blackouts did I realize my true powerlessness. One day I awoke from a blackout to find myself in the operating room, standing over the open abdomen of a patient I did not know, doing I knew not what. I asked my assistant to finish the case and ran to the scrub room where I threw up and started to cry. I had to come close to killing somebody before I realized how sick I was. My partner intervened on me later that day and took me to my first AA meeting."

"I want you to go back to your apartments now for a special A. A. meeting, and I want you to discuss the concept of powerlessness. I want you to preface every sharing with the words…I was so powerless over my drug that I … and fill in the blank with concrete examples of how your addiction controls your life. Rest assured that you will make no headway in this program until you are absolutely convinced of your powerlessness in the face of drink and drug."

Back in the apartment, we were joined by a few of the fellows from next door.

Jimmy took a very deep breath before speaking.

"I was so powerless over my addiction that I used skunk water to inject my meth. Near the end of my using, I would stop along the road and shoot up every day on the way to work. One morning I forgot the saline I used to dilute the drug. In a panic, I pulled over near a drainage ditch. I dipped stagnant water out of the ditch and used it to inject my drug. I could have cared less about the germs and poisons I was injecting into my heart, as long as I got high." Jimmy paused and looked around the room as if in a daze. "My God," he said. "I can't believe I did that."

"Last ditch," said Robert, suppressing a laugh.

"I'd been up late, shooting cocaine," I said, taking my turn. "I gathered up all the dirty needles, put them in a garbage bag, then threw the bag outside. The next morning was sunny, it was springtime, and I could hear the birds singing. Life was good. Then I walked past the garbage bag on my way to the car. Suddenly, without thinking, I ripped open the bag, hoping to find a syringe that had cocaine left in it. I found two syringes partially filled with cocaine and mixed with blood that had turned a rancid brown. I was so powerless over my addiction that I rolled up my sleeves and injected myself with the dirty needles, not once but twice. But the cocaine's get-highs had died in the night. I didn't even get a buzz, although I got blood all over my tie."

"Makes sense to me," said Mike.

We were standing in the smoking pit behind the client lounge, waiting for the next session to start. The smoke was curling around the head of a newcomer named Charles. He seemed lost in reverie. Charles was an orthopedic surgeon who had become addicted to pain pills, which he took avidly. But his real love was cocaine, and he was not shy about sticking a needle in his arm and shooting the drug into his veins.

"It's faster that way," he said. "I started out snorting at parties, but pretty soon Lady Cocaine and I were best buddies." He grinned.

"I've done a little cocaine myself," I admitted.

"Oh, boy," he began. "I can remember ... Maybe I shouldn't tell this."

Robert sauntered up. "Our secrets will destroy us. Better fess up."

My curiosity was killing me. What had the richest orthopod in Sarasota done to party down?

"Okay," he said. "My wife and I had been doing coke, wine, and pot all evening, and by midnight I was blitzed beyond sanity. We both had to work the next day, so I wasn't surprised when she said matter-of-factly, That's all the cocaine you can have tonight. She was in charge of hiding the stash and I had no idea where it was. Then something strange happened."

"Do tell," said Robert, all ears.

"I can't remember exactly what happened, but suddenly I was nine feet tall and stood looming over my wife. I picked her up and threw her bodily to the floor. I stood over her, ripped off my wedding ring, and threw it in her face. I cursed her using all the tender words that usually accompanied our lovemaking. I roared and I mean I really roared. The curtains shook from the blast." He paused and took a drag off his cigarette.

"The next thing I knew," he said, "I was cowering in the corner while the beast stood over her. I was scared to death that he would come after me next. He was huge, angry, and murderous. When he looked in my direction, I could see he was gloating. If he came at me, I knew I would be dead meat."

Robert and I both stared unbelievingly.

"But you know what," he said, "all the time I knew the monster was me. I know that hidden inside me was a beast trying to break out of my subconscious. I've never been so afraid in all my life. I told Cameron I would do anything rather than have the monster return. I knew that the next time he could kill somebody, maybe me."

"That's the reason you came to rehab?" asked Robert.

"I hate to admit it, but yes," said Charles. "I really didn't care that cocaine was ruining my life, but the thought of this beast emerging and overwhelming me—I'm willing to do whatever it takes to prevent that from happening again."

Andrew, a cardiologist from West Virginia, was up next.

"I was so powerless over my disease that I abandoned my professional ethics," he said, head down. "I got a call at about 3 am. from the hospital. My usual practice was to see each new admission whenever they hit the ER, no matter what time it was. I couldn't conscience prescribing therapy for someone I hadn't personally examined. But that night I was blisteringly high on bourbon and meth and was bedding two nurses at the same time.

It was incredible. And I wasn't about to let anything interfere with my fun. The ER physician was very enabling. No need for you to come in this late, he said. I'll write a set of holding orders for Mr. Sams until you can see him in the morning."

"I hung up and immediately forgot about Mr. Sams and his heart attack. Just before dawn, my debauchery was interrupted by another phone call. A nurse on the Cardiac Unit was calling with an update. Mr. Sams' condition was deteriorating. I said as little as possible to hide my slurred speech. The family is here and would like to speak to you, she said. I nodded through the telephone but hung up anyway. Back to bed, whispered my little blonde hussy."

"Two hours later the phone rang again. Mr. Sams died a few minutes ago, said the nurse. I took a deep breath but said nothing recognizable. 'He was pretty far gone when he got here,' she said. 'There wasn't much you could have done. The family has already gone home.'

"By the time my head hit the pillow, I had again forgotten all about Mr. Sams and his heart. That morning I called the office. I had a rough night at the hospital, I told them. Reschedule all my appointments for today, will ya?"

"I was so powerless over my addiction," whispered Mike, "that I abandoned my principles."

Crossing the Line

"Good morning," said Cameron. "Today, we're going to talk about crossing the line. Anyone know what that means?"

Mike raised his hand. "The line that separates the men from the boys."

"Uh, no," said Cameron, laughing. "I'm talking about the line that separates abuse from addiction. Just using a lot of drugs or booze doesn't make me an addict. What's the difference?"

"Someone who uses a lot of drugs can still quit when they want," said Robert. "But guys like me and Mike have lost that ability. Once we pick up the first drink, we can't stop until we pass out or run out of booze."

Vera said, "It seems to me, using is a choice. My cousin can decide if he wants to get drunk or stoned. He has the capacity to choose. But for me, when I crossed that line, I lost the power of choice. Now, I have a disease, the disease of addiction, and when the craving hits me, I'm no longer in control. I can't be comfortable in my own skin until I have a drink inside me. Then, of course, I can't stop."

"The Old Timers says it's like turning a grape into a raisin," said Mike. "A raisin can never go back to being a grape again."

"Or a cucumber into a pickle," said a voice from the back of the room.

"Our disease has a lot in common with another chronic disease, diabetes," Cameron said. "A person isn't born with diabetes, but they can inherit the predisposition from their parents. The disease may never express itself. But at some point, if that invisible line is crossed, a person's body can no longer handle sugar. For the rest of their lives, they'll be diabetic. No matter how long or how well they control their blood sugar, if they stop their medication, the disease will return."

"Addiction appears to be inherited as well," she continued. "It may skip generations. It may be expressed as dependence on drugs and alcohol, or as other behaviors like shoplifting or gambling."

"My parents smoked, but weren't addicted to anything else," I said. "But I have cousins on both sides with addictive behavior. One's already died."

"I don't remember crossing any line," said Mike. "My descent into the bottle was slow and gradual. Looking back, I have no clear idea of when I lost control."

"But you did," I said. Mike nodded.

"Once across that line," said Cameron, "the complications of the disease become apparent. I will no longer be able to drink socially. I become susceptible to every get-high you can name. My behavior will begin to change and negative consequences start to accumulate."

"Once I cross the line, I can never go back," said Mike. "I've lost all control over my using. Where once I could take it or leave it, now I can only take it. I'll never again be able to drink like a normal person. For the rest of my life, I'll be an alcoholic."

Shit, I said to myself. I had secretly been holding on to the idea that one day I would be able to drug and drink like I used to, before the bottom fell out. Maybe they were right, probably they were right, but in the far back of my mind, I could feel the lingering hope still there, just out of reach.

The craving and the allergy

Taylor was lecturing to the assembled drunks and junkies, easily a hundred of us there in the auditorium. He began by reading from a book.

"'We believe that the action of alcohol on chronic alcoholics is a manifestation of an allergy; that the phenomenon of craving is limited to this class and never occurs in the average temperate drinker. These allergic types can never safely use alcohol in any form at all; and once having formed the habit and found they cannot break it, once having lost their self-confidence, their reliance upon things human, their problems pile up on them and become astonishingly difficult to solve. Frothy emotional appeal seldom suffices. The message which can interest and hold these alcoholic people must have depth and weight. In nearly all cases, their ideals must be grounded in a power greater than themselves, if they are to recreate their lives.' That's a quote from the Big Book of AA."

"Once we cross over the line into addiction, two changes occur. The first is known as craving, the second is the allergy. The changes are permanent and do not occur in Earth people. Craving is a deeply emotional and irrational desire for using. It may occur at any time and without warning. It may arise from the worst kind of magical thinking. It can be triggered by the presence of old playmates, old playgrounds, and old playthings. Once the craving begins, we can find no relief until we pick up our drug of choice."

"Immediately after the first sip or line or toke, the phenomenon of "allergy" begins. AA describes it as an allergy to alcohol, but not in the sense of allergy to ragweed or seasonal allergens. Rather, something about our body chemistry is different. One drink inevitably leads to another in a completely uncontrollable cascade."

Taylor picked up the Big Book again and began to read. "I do not hold with those who believe that alcoholism is entirely a problem of mental control. I have had many men who had, for example, worked a period of months on some problem or business deal which was to be settled on a certain date, favorably to them. They took a drink a day or so prior to the date, and then the phenomenon of craving at once became paramount to all other interests so that the important appointment was not met. These men were not drinking to escape; they were drinking to overcome a craving beyond their mental control. It has never been, by any treatment with which we are familiar, permanently eradicated. The only relief we have to suggest is entire abstinence.'" He put the book down.

"Our disease is not due to a lack of willpower or poor moral standards. It is part of the insanity of our disease, which tells us that this time, we'll be able to drink or drug normally and get away with it. The thought of the possible consequences is driven from our minds. This is far more than just Jones-ing. The craving becomes an unstoppable force that no normal person can understand. The craving is beyond our best mental control and it can only be satisfied when our drug of choice finally enters our body. Normal people have no such response to the first drink. They can have two martinis and go home. But for us, the only way to avoid this chain of events is not to take that first drink. This is what they mean when they say, "one drink is too many and a thousand is never enough."

Sitting in the back of the room, I felt his words around me, like a thin winter coat, small protection from the storm of my cravings. But for the first time, my uncontrollable urges were beginning to make sense.

The turd cycle

Cameron had the afternoon off, so Carl, a psychologist on staff, took her place. Carl was known for pontificating at times, but he knew a lot about living and was good at sharing it.

"Today, we're going to talk about the turd cycle," he said. Laughter moved around the room and Carl smiled.

"No, really," he said. "As a child, my daddy repeatedly called me Little Turd. After hearing those words over and over, I came to believe him and I started to act accordingly. Those around me said, Carl acts like a little turd, and they began treating me like a little turd. Of course, I felt their disregard and I was sure that my dad's assessment was correct. I was a little turd, it was my place in life, and I kept acting that way. The self-fulfilling prophecy of childhood. So goes the turd cycle."

"To change someone's behavior, intervention usually occurs at the point of their perception of themselves. As long as I believe that I'm a little turd, I'll keep acting like a little turd. Only if my self-image changes will my behavior change. If I'm repeatedly told that I'm not a little turd but actually a fine upstanding young man, eventually I'll become convinced of my self-worth. With a change in the way I perceive myself, my behavior will change, and because if I believe I'm a good person, I'll act accordingly. Those around me will begin to think, Carl acts like a fine and worthy person. We must have been mistaken in our assessment of him. Then they begin treating me with respect. I'll sense this and begin to think, maybe I'm a good person after all. With the change in my self-image, my behavior has changed. The negative cycle that ruled my life has been broken.

"But for the alcoholic and addict, this process doesn't work," he said. "The addict's thinker is broken. His brain has been pickled by drugs and booze. Stuck inside his fixed opinions and hiding behind his denial, he won't listen to new ideas. A change in his life must come at the next step in the cycle, that of behavior. He must first learn to act sober, even if his mind refuses to accept the tenets of recovery. Like a recruit on the parade ground, he must practice his new behavior over and over, because instilling new behavior doesn't occur quickly."

"With time, abstinence will bring a measure of sanity. Their perception of themselves in the world will improve and their new behavior is reinforced, and they will find vindication from others. New thinking will follow, and the cycle will be broken. Because of the depth of his insanity, however, the cycle must be repeated many, many times before his thinking will clear. That's why the process of recovery takes so long to be successful. Certainly, much longer than twenty-eight days."

Leon leaned over and whispered: "Fake it til you make it."

"Yup," I said, wondering how long my cycling would take.

Relapsing disease

Vera, Mike, and I were at an AA meeting near rehab. Carol was the speaker this night. She was dressed in used clothes, her arms were a patchwork of fading tattoos, but there was a light in her eyes.

"I'm forty-eight now," she began. "When I was eight, I started drinking the leftovers from my parents' parties. By thirteen I was drinking every day. My older sister took me to my first AA meeting when I was fifteen, but it was just a bunch of old geezers smoking cigarettes, so I didn't pay it no mind. By eighteen I was trading sex for cocaine and heroin. I almost died from overdoses twice, so I went over to vodka. I used to keep three maybe four gallons in the freezer all the time. It's better when it's really cold."

We laughed with her. She continued.

"I picked up my first white chip when I was twenty-five. Social Service took away my baby because I was an unfit mother. I was pregnant with my second before I tried to quit for real. I stayed sober for almost eighteen months, but my old man showed up with a bag of dope and I was off and running. It was seven years before I picked up another beginner's chip. My kids were living with my mother and she had a court order out against me so I couldn't see them. I got a job working as a waitress and made pretty good money. I even bought a car. Then my roommate came home with a new drug she called crack and I learned to smoke the crack pipe. Gave my car to the dope man. Spent nine months in Butner for depression and drugs. Stayed sober most of that time but was drinking again as soon as I got out."

She paused and looked up at the ceiling before continuing.

"I was at the end of my rope, ready to kill myself, when somebody steered me to a halfway recovery house. I lived there with a bunch of women who were trying to get sober for themselves. I tried getting sober to get my kids back, but that didn't work. I tried getting sober to make my mom proud of me, but that didn't work neither. Now I'm sober for myself, so I can have a real life. Today I have a job, my own place, and I get to see my kids every weekend." She grinned, the light shining in her eyes. "Today, and just for today, I'm sober."

We all clapped and cheered.

Cross-addiction

I was almost a month sober when I first heard someone say he was cross-addicted. He said he was a heroin addict and that now he was cross-addicted to alcohol.

I wondered what he meant by cross-addiction and why he was different from everyone else in the room. But the explanation, it turned out, was that we are all cross-addicted, and not just to one drug, but to all the get-highs you can name. We were in Cameron's classroom.

"Once we crossed that invisible line that leads to addiction," she said, "I'm susceptible to all drugs and get-highs, even if I've never used them before. That is cross-addiction."

"Failure to appreciate this has led to more than one relapse. A famous actor, who had been clean and sober for twenty years, was given hydrocodone for low back pain. For most people, this wouldn't have been a problem. But the hydrocodone rekindled his addiction and he was found dead with a needle in his arm from an overdose of heroin."

"Just because a narcotic or benzodiazepine is prescribed for an appropriate medical reason doesn't protect us. A good friend, a recovering opioid addict undergoing gall bladder surgery, was given intravenous morphine by pump post-operatively. She could use a button to tell the pump when to give an extra dose. Fifteen years of sobriety and a full kit of spiritual tools did not prevent her from relapsing."

"We must become unrelenting advocates for our own sobriety. In preparation for a medical procedure, I told two doctors, three nurses, and one anesthesiologist that I could not take narcs or benzos. A second anesthesiologist showed up carrying two syringes ready to inject me with both. Are you ready for the good stuff? he joked. To me, it was not a joke."

"I don't like pain," said John, sitting beside me. "But I like relapse even less. Give me Tylenol and ibuprofen but let me stay sober."

Changeable addictions

Mike and I were heading across town to a detox facility in north Atlanta. By meeting and counseling the alcoholics and addicts there, we were supposed to see a reflection of ourselves in them. As we drove, we shared stories of our families and their encounters with addiction.

"My grandfather ran moonshine across the ridges of Harlan County, at least until he got religion," said Mike. "He became a preacher of the Holy Word, even ran for county judge. My father would drive him to four or five tent meetings a day. He preached at revivals, on the radio, and on TV. You hated to see him coming because you knew he was going to preach at you until your ears turned red."

"A real foot-washing, hellfire-and-brimstone kinda guy," I said.

"Truly. I've always believed that he swapped alcoholism for his own personal brand of hyper-religiosity."

"A bunch of guys here have swapped addictions, too," I said. "Like Bobby, the New Hampshire dentist—a heroin addict who gave up the needle for Kentucky bourbon. Now he gets drunk every night."

"I met a businessman at a meeting in Buckhead," Mike said. "Told me he was a real alcoholic. After he quit drinking, he found himself working 10, 12, even 14 hours a day. He asked me if I thought he'd just traded addictions."

"Probably," I said. "You know about James, don't you? A full professor of medicine at the university whose pleasure was self-administered Demerol. He gave up the needle and started smoking unfiltered Camels."

Mike laughed. "There's a guy named Wimpy, a dentist in my morning group. He's a fan of Demerol, too. His other addiction is buying VHS tapes! He shops secretively at the video store, hides the tapes under his coat until he gets to the counter then pays for them surreptitiously. When he gets home, he hurries downstairs so no one will know what he's doing and puts them up on a shelf in his study. He has a whole wall full of them. He never actually watches the movies, only buys them addictively and sneaks them home."

"We're a strange group," I said. "I know of a famous Hollywood actress who was arrested for compulsive shoplifting. She apologized in court, but the judge sentenced her to drug abuse treatment."

"My buddy Dan is an emergency room doc from Sacramento. He loves the crack pipe. His sister's addiction is bulimia—another form. There was a guy in morning group who admitted to masturbating fifty times a day. Somehow he managed to hold down a full-time job."

We pulled into the driveway at detox.

"One last story," I said. "Big Jed is a bad meth freak. He grinds his teeth all day long."

"Yep," said Mike. "He told me he ground down his natural teeth and two pairs of dentures. Picked up his habit after being discharged from the service with PTSD, a problem for a lot of us."

"We're a decidedly unusual group," I said.

"Decidedly," he said. "If it changes the way I feel and I can do it twice, I can become addicted to it."

Worldwide prevalence

At lunch the next day, Mike pointed out the new fish sitting across the cafeteria.

"Johnny Red Hawk. Pediatrician," said Mike. "He's a Cherokee Indian."

"Not only that, he's a medicine man," I said. "He's in my morning group. He told me that almost half of his relatives are alcoholics! That seems like a lot. He said it was because of his Indian blood."

"He's right, you know," said Reggie. "Taylor said that across the board ten percent of the world's population is addicted, right? The only exception is the American Indian, where it's forty percent."

"That old saw about Indians and firewater is true?" I asked.

"I'm not sure I'd go that far," said Mike, waving at Johnny, who waved back. Mike returned to his dessert.

"Taylor also said that there are three times as many men as women in AA," I said.

"Yes," mumbled Mike through his pie, "and you'd better not get caught fraternizing with any of them."

Family abuse

After lunch, we walked back to rehab for the afternoon session. Mike stubbed out his cigarette and we went inside.

"Somewhere I got the idea that real alcoholics came from abusive homes, but that doesn't seem to be the case," I said.

"Taylor says only about a third of us come from bad family backgrounds," said Mike, "which means almost seventy percent of us come from relatively normal families."

"My childhood was as much like that TV show 'The Waltons' as possible," I said. "Maybe with a little 'Ozzie and Harriet' thrown in. My parents didn't drink, gamble, run around, or anything like that. I had a perfect childhood."

Mike shook his head. "That's not what you said in group this morning."

"I don't know what you mean," I answered.

"You said that when you were fifteen, your younger brother died of leukemia. A year later, your father died of a heart attack at the ripe old age of thirty-eight. I think that might qualify as an abused childhood."

"I never thought about it that way. I guess I did take a hit, didn't I?"

"No denying it," said my friend Mike.

Hereditary nature

Later that day, Mike and I were at Fulton County Detox. We drove there twice a week to lead a class on alcoholism and addiction. Mike was explaining the inherited nature of our disease.

Alicia, who never met a crack pipe she didn't like, looked puzzled.

"I don't understand," she said in a soft Southern drawl. "Both my parents are alcoholics, but us kids are all crackheads. How can that be running in the family, like he said?"

Driving back, Mike said that when he was admitted to rehab, his family was shocked. "None of us ever had this kind of problem, they said." He laughed. "Last night I was talking with my cousin Louise, who's living out of her car."

Mike shared his conversation with Louise.

"I can't believe you're living in your car," I said to her. "Where do you park it?"

"Right now, I'm in my daughter's driveway," Louise replied. "She won't let me in her house, but then neither will my other daughter. At least I still have my cell phone so I can check my email."

"You know," I said, "I'm beginning to think addiction runs in our family."

"Oh, hell yes," she said. "My dad was a workaholic who drank himself silly. I'm sure our uncle Lyndon was a closet drunk, and I went to rehab for twenty-eight days back in the '90s for my Xanax problem. And you know about our cousin Tina, she was a terrible drunk, died of cirrhosis before she was thirty-two."

"Neither of my parents drank or gambled or any of that stuff," I said. "Maybe it skips generations."

"Could be," said his cousin. "Anyway, we sure got it."

"Amen to that," I said.

"When I was admitted to detox," I told Mike, "my family acted surprised that I had a problem with drugs and alcohol. No one in our family has ever had *that* before. But since then, I've learned of at least six cousins, on both sides of the family, who have serious problems with addiction. And quite a few are bipolar, too."

Outcomes: death

Abe B. was a long-time friend of Dr. Taylor and once a year he would come down from Hazelden to give us the benefits of his experience in dealing with drunks and junkies.

"Left untreated, there are only three outcomes of addiction," he said. "Jails, institutions, and death. Let's start with death. Some will die of an overdose. Others will die of the toxic effects of alcohol on the major organs: the heart, (cardiomyopathy), the liver (cirrhosis), or the pancreas (pancreatitis). Every year some teenager shows off by downing a fifth of Jack Daniels in one gulp and ends up dying in the ER of acute alcoholic poisoning. But death takes other forms as well. Let me tell you about Jeremy."

"Jeremy was a family practice doc from Baltimore. He was a little guy with mousy brown hair and a quiet personality. He smiled a lot and everybody liked him. His drinking problem led him to rehab with us up in Minnesota. He worked hard at the recovery path laid out in front of him. He shared his problems, went to meetings, worked the steps, and did everything he was asked to do. He was a model recovery person.

On the day he left rehab, we held a going-away party for him at a local Italian restaurant. We toasted each other with iced tea over plates of spaghetti and laughed and felt good about how recovery was saving all our lives. He left with a smile on his face.

A week later one of my counselors pulled me aside and told me that Jeremy was dead. A week after he left rehab, he walked off the balcony of a ten-story building."

"Then there was Reuben." He stopped and sighed visibly. "Reuben was an I.V. drug addict and alcoholic who had been clean and sober for over ten years. For the last five, he had run a recovery house outside Eau Claire. He was in a good place. The promises of AA had all come true for him, and he lived a grateful and happy life."

"Then, for no apparent reason, he lost his appetite and began losing weight. Unknown to him, more than ten years before, he had contracted Hepatitis C from his drug use. The virus only manifested itself when it triggered the development of liver cancer. He was dead in three months."

"Eric was a friend of mine from my days at the University of Chicago Med. We attended AA meetings together and he had a successful career as a radiologist. His son, Greg, was as fond of drugs as his dad had been of his wine. Greg's drug of choice was the speedball, a combination of heroin and cocaine, injected, often with a dirty needle. For some reason, one of the consequences of speedballs is subacute bacterial endocarditis, where bacterial colonies form on the valves of the heart. Once embedded in the valves, they are all but impossible to get rid of. The infected valves shed clumps of bacteria that settle anywhere in the body causing strokes, pneumonia, kidney failure, and more. In Greg's case, the infection settled in his brain causing seizures. As the germs multiplied in his head, his brain literally melted. Eric had to watch his son die a slow and agonizing death. Eric was devastated. Losing a child may be the worst thing that can happen to a human being, but Eric didn't drink over the tragedy."

Outcomes: institutions

Robert, Vera, and I were hanging out in the courtyard after lunch when Wee Willy walked up.

"Hiya, dudes," he said in his deep Irish brogue. "How's it hangin'?" Wee Willy was from Dublin, a podiatrist by trade, in Atlanta looking for sobriety. He was small and impish, and the first time I saw him and heard his delightful accent, I knew he had to be a leprechaun.

"Hello," Vera said. "What's new?"

The Irishman frowned. "Just heard from home. My best uncle died last week. He was in a home for the feeble-minded."

"I'm sorry to hear that," said Robert.

"Uncle Mick was a good drinking buddy," said Wee Willy, "but I ain't seen 'im in years. They say he lost his mind. One day he was taking the trolley home and couldn't remember his stop. They found him in a city park, crying. Wasn't long before they were feeding him through a tube. He was only forty-two."

"Sounds pretty awful," I said.

"That's not the worst of it." He grinned. "Being here, I'm gonna miss his wake. My family throws one helluva party. In honor of the deceased, I mean."

After Wee Willy wandered off, Vera said, "Wet brain."

"Huh?" I asked.

"Wet brain. You know, when alcohol rots your brain from the inside out. Booze is toxic to the nerve cells and slowly kills them off. It's one form of dementia, but around here they just call it wet brain. Starts with memory loss, progresses to global cognitive dysfunction, and you end up in an institution unable to take care of yourself."

I flashed on a memory of a day in my clinic, when I couldn't remember the product of 8 times 12. I had downed an excessive amount of wine the night before, even for me. At the time I wondered if my drinking was beginning to affect my memory, but I dismissed the thought as silly. Stuff like that didn't happen to me, I was a doctor. Now, I'm not so sure.

Outcomes: jails and prisons

We were having dinner and a group AA meeting in Robert's apartment. He was grilling hamburgers and corn-on-the-cob. Not known for his skill in the kitchen, nonetheless, he did cook a mean burger.

After eating, we gathered to hear Charles tell his story. Dr. Taylor had rescued him from the Federal Penitentiary in Atlanta. The orthopedic surgeon had been self-prescribing pain pills. By the time the DEA hauled him in, he was taking over two hundred pills a day. The DEA was sure he was dealing. They couldn't remotely imagine that he was taking that many pills himself. Dr. Taylor got wind of his story, pulled a few strings, and had him transferred to rehab. If he could complete the program here, the authorities were willing to cut him some slack. Failure meant going back to jail.

"It all started when I hurt my back," said Charles. "My family doc gave me hydrocodone. When the pain left, I kept taking the pills because I liked the way they made me feel. When my doc wouldn't give me any more pills, I went doctor shopping and got prescriptions from six different physicians, but eventually they quit prescribing too. That's when I began writing prescriptions for myself, filling them at different pharmacies around town so I wouldn't be noticed. I mean, what's the problem, eh? I wasn't hurting anybody. I just needed my pills to keep going. But I musta hit one pharmacy one time too many."

"You didn't think you could keep doing that forever, did you?" I asked.

"That was the problem," Charles said. "I didn't think."

"What're you going to do now?" Robert asked.

"Whatever it takes to stay out of the slammer," said Charles.

After dinner, Robert and I spoke.

"You know," Robert said, "staying out of jail isn't sufficient motivation to get sober. It doesn't work. You can't get sober to get your job back, your family, or your pickup truck back. You have to get sober for yourself."

Charles left rehab eventually with the blessings of the staff but was picked up six months later by the DEA. He had come up with a new scheme to buy his drugs wholesale from overseas, but the law was two steps ahead of him. He was facing eight years of hard time in the Big House.

The functional alcoholic

It was mid-morning and we were assembled in the classroom for a lecture by Dr. Taylor.

"When I was younger and just learning about my own drinking problem, I went to New York and interviewed dozens of drunks on the street and in the burned-out buildings of the Bowery. It was amazing how intelligent these guys were. Turned out, most of them were lawyers."

Mike leaned over and whispered, "Makes sense to me."

"Most of us," said Dr. Taylor, "go to work every day, bring home or squander our paychecks, and somehow survive in the world. Only at the very end of our drinking do we end up sleeping under a bridge or waiting in a soup line. It may take twenty or thirty years of hard drinking to put a man on the street."

"With cocaine, it only took me eighteen months," I whispered to Robert.

"Good work," said Robert, under his breath. "Very efficient use of time."

Abstinence isn't enough

The overcast sky had lifted, and the afternoon sun was warm on my face. Timmy and I were sitting on the cool grass behind the apartments, enjoying a day without drugs.

"With your superior intelligence I'm surprised you weren't asked to run for King of the Universe," Timmy said, grinning. "I hear the position may be coming open soon."

"You're so cute," I said. "But you know, they say a dry drunk would make a perfect King of the World."

"What's a dry drunk?" said Timmy.

"Well, a dry drunk is an alcoholic who, for whatever reason, quits drinking. He loses the chemical coping that booze provides but hasn't developed sufficient non-chemical coping skills to deal with life. He's achingly uncomfortable in his own skin. You remember when we visited Big Jed's family?"

A few weeks ago, Timmy, Mike, and I visited Big Jed's parents. Big Jed's mom was the most gracious and genuine of Southern hostesses. She had cooked a huge Southern-style turkey dinner with all the trimmings. George, Big Jed's dad, was a real honest-to-goodness rocket scientist at McDonnell-Douglas. Big Jed's parents seemed exceptionally normal until after dinner.

"When I was in college," said George, the workaholic aerospace engineer, "I tried drinking beer, but I liked it so much I knew I'd better leave it alone."

As he spoke of his son's problems with meth, his hands gripped the arms of his chair.

"I can't stand spending all that money for Jed's rehab. It really galls me," he said. "I can't believe those people know what they're doing. Don't get me wrong, I love my son, but he sure costs me a lot of money."

"You design experimental planes?" I asked, trying to change the subject.

"Yeah, I'm part of a team of twenty engineers," he replied, "so you might think the big wigs would listen to me. I do all the damn work and those guys take all the credit. Those guys never had an original idea in their whole life. If it weren't for me, nothing would ever get done."

His hands were gripping the arms of his chair so tightly that his knuckles were white.

Back at the apartments, Mike said "I think Big Jed's dad may be a dry drunk. He seems to have all the problems of an alcoholic, just not the drinking. You saw him white-knuckling the arms of his chair?"

"Yup," I said. "He works at least ten hours a day and brings his work home every night. He is addicted to his job just like his son is addicted to crystal meth. Being an aerospace dude is more important to him than anything else. And he knows he could do a better job running the world if people would only listen to him."

"We found relief with better chemistry," said Mike.

"I'm in favor of chemistry, as long as it includes Ritalin," said Timmy.

"But now we have a better way," Mike said.

Timmy just smiled.

It was Eldon's first day in rehab. He was tall, thin, and grayish, with a paunch, a preacher from a small town in the panhandle of Florida. In the cafeteria at lunch, Robert spotted him and grabbed Reggie and me and we sat down next to him.

"Hello, Eldon," said Reggie, reaching for the salt.

"Hi," said Eldon grudgingly. "Sit down."

"We did," said Robert, maintaining a grin. "Would you care to join us?"

"I have," said Eldon, managing the barest of smiles.

"You might try the salmon," said Robert. "It's really terrible here."

"It does make me want to puke," said Eldon, pushing his plate away.

"I do, however, recommend the apple pie," said Robert, staring at the uneaten pie on Eldon's tray. "It's good for the spirit."

Eldon was decidedly unhappy. He looked like he was about to explode.

"You know, Eldon," I said, "when I got here, they told me I had to get rid of all my resentments if I wanted to find any of peace."

"I don't have any resentments," he said, glaring at me. "I just hate everybody."

"Isn't that a form of resentment?" I asked.

"Oh, go f— yourself," Eldon cursed. He threw his fork down and bolted from the cafeteria.

"Too bad. He forgot his dessert," said Robert, reaching for the pie.

That evening, Reggie was cooking supper for us, rice and beans with cornbread. Eldon sat on the couch, his jaw clenched. He sighed, rubbed his head with one hand, then sighed again.

"Would you like a drink, Eldon?" asked Reggie.

"Boy, would I," said Eldon. "What've you got? I thought we weren't allowed to drink here. I sure could use a shot of bourbon."

"No bourbon," Reggie's smiled. "Just iced tea."

Eldon's eyes rolled back in his head and he chuckled. "Should've known," he said. "And I thought you guys were hard drinkers like me."

"We are, preacher," I said, "but we don't have to do it anymore."

"I don't have to," he said, "I just want to."

"Are you angry?" asked Robert. "Sounds like you might be angry."

"I'm a pastor in the Methodist church," he said. "How could I possibly be angry?"

"Cause we drunks is always gettin' angry 'bout something'," I said.

"Well, I don't think I feel angry," said Eldon.

"But you do look just a mite uncomfortable," Robert said, giggling. "Restless, irritable, and discontent is what they call it around here. So...." Robert waved his hands around in the air, looking for the right word, "so, stressed out you could bust. Or get drunk. Right?"

Eldon was silent.

"What brought you here, Reverend?" I asked. "And don't tell me it was the taxi."

"Ha, ha, that's so funny," said Eldon. "If you must know, the wife of the head deacon made an unfair accusation against me."

"Which was?" Reggie asked, serving up plates of food.

"She said I was having an affair with her," Eldon's anger was rising.

"And were you?" I asked.

"Of course, I was," shouted Eldon, standing up, "but it was unfair of her to say so."

Reggie held out a plate for Eldon. Eldon smashed it with his fist and stomped from the room.

The next morning Eldon was no better.

"Good morning, Eldon," said Matt, as we settled down for his session.

Eldon just glowered.

"I guess anger is as good a topic as any," said Matt. "What's the cause of our anger?"

"I can answer this one," Timmy said, forgetting himself and standing up. "We're angry because we're afraid."

"Afraid of what?" asked Matt.

"Robert told me that I have three basic fears," said Timmy. "One, I'm afraid of losing what I have. Two, I'm afraid of not getting what I want. And three, I'm afraid that if you really knew who I was, you wouldn't like me. Robert said, these fears drive my ego and generate all my character defects. They prevent me from finding any real sense of peace."

"Very good, Timmy," said Matt. "You may sit down now. Vera, how does your fear control you?"

"Before I got here, I didn't think I was scared of anything," said Vera, "But now I know that's not exactly true. My fear makes me want to control the world around me. I try to manipulate people, places, and things to get what I want. Somewhere I got the idea that if I can control the outer world, I'll control the chaos inside my head."

"How did that work for you?" asked Matt.

"Not very well," said Vera. "Like Eldon, I ended up here."

That afternoon, we were sitting on the breezeway watching Mike smoke a cigarette when Eldon walked by.

"Preacher," said Reggie, "why don't you pull up a chair and stay awhile. Or maybe a month or two."

"I can't possibly stay here for two months," said Eldon, his eyes like daggers. "I've got business to take care of. Two months—no way."

"I've learned that I shouldn't put limits on my recovery," said Reggie.

"I can't make it without my Scotch," said Eldon. "That's all there is to it." He rolled his eyes at Reggie. "How can you possibly wake up in the morning and realize this is the best you're going to feel all day."

"I'm not so sure about that," said Robert. "You're capable of much more than you can possibly imagine."

"You can ask God for help," said Reggie softly.

"God! What God?" Eldon was boiling now. "He never showed up when I needed him. Never answered my prayers. Couldn't be bothered with the likes of me."

"If I limit my Higher Power," Reggie said, "I only limit myself."

"I just can't see it," said Eldon with unexpected honesty. "I'm gonna keep on drinking no matter what you do or say."

"What?" I asked.

"I'm trapped," Eldon repeated. "Stuck. There's no way I'll ever be able to quit."

Matt's words came back to me: If I feel trapped in the circumstances of my life, it is only my disease talking. Life is always about choices.

Within an hour, Eldon had packed his bags, thrown them in the back of his aging Chevrolet station wagon, and driven off. We never saw or heard from him again.

"Don't put limits on yourself, your recovery, or your Higher Power," said Robert as we walked to the center the next morning.

Addiction is a Disease

Using is a choice, but addiction is a disease.

An alcoholic is the same as an addict.

I am a good person with a bad disease.

I am uncomfortable in my own skin. I will do anything to change the way I feel.

Addiction is a chronic, relapsing, and fatal disease.

Addiction takes control of all aspects of my life and I am powerless to change.

An invisible line separates a user from an addict. Once over the line, I can never go back.

The irrational and unexpected craving for my drug of choice cannot be resisted.

Once across the line into addiction, we are susceptible to all the get-highs you can name.

Addiction takes many forms, from hyper-religiosity, gambling, to compulsive shoplifting, and more.

Alcoholic Insanity

*"During these fits of absolute unconsciousness I drank,
God only knows how often or how much.
As a matter of course my enemies referred the insanity to the drink
rather than the drink to the insanity."*
—Edgar Allan Poe

Disordered thinking

Dr. Taylor's friend Abe G. was giving his second lecture, this time about the disordered thinking that characterizes our disease.

"It's been years since I was in rehab," he said. "They told my counselor that I was "stone crazy." If you'd asked me, I would've said that my thinking was quite normal. It was a long time before I realized that I had the condition called the insanity of alcoholism. Stinking Thinking, they said it was."

"As the degree of my using worsened, so did my grip on reality. My slide into full-blown alcoholism was so gradual that I didn't notice that my mental function was deteriorating as well. Everybody else could see it, but not me. I was blind to what was happening. Maybe I didn't want to know."

"Thoughts and actions that would seem crazy to regular people, became everyday happenings. For example, it's normal to hide my booze and drugs around the house, so they'll always be there when I need them. It's normal to hide my empty whiskey bottles in the dumpster down the street so no one would know how much I'm drinking. It's a good thing to drink a lot before I left the house, so I wouldn't have to worry about getting enough later. Should I hide my car keys so I won't get another DUI? Doesn't everyone carry miniatures of whiskey in their socks for emergencies when taking the family out to dinner? And so on."

"A hundred forms of negativity came to dominate my thoughts: fear, low self-esteem, resentments, anger, paranoia, and more. My logic had become completely screwed—of course it was normal to drive down the road with a needle in your arm shooting cocaine, yeah! Hey, forget about seeing your kids on the weekend, let's get high instead! Honest? —of course, I'm honest, I only steal as much as I need. And so forth."

"As my mental sickness worsened, my brain filtered out anything which interfered with my addiction. I didn't hear the warnings of my friends. I ignored the damage that was happening to my body. I ignored what my conscience was telling me."

"I learned to dismiss anything that remotely threatened my using. I could instantly forget the warning the cop just gave me about driving and drinking. I could forget my boss telling me for the last time to quit drinking or he'd fire me."

He paused and wiped his brow, looking out over his audience as if looking deep into his memoried past.

"I slowly became the person I swore I'd never to be. I was becoming my father."

My father had been kind and good. He never drank, never cheated on my mother, or committed any dishonesty I could remember. Why couldn't I want to grow up to be like him? I didn't get it.

The insanity of addiction

"I like you guys and girls a lot, but really, you're all completely insane," said Cameron. She walked back and forth in front of the blackboard then turned. "You," she pointed her finger straight at me. "are insane in oh-so-many ways."

In my bewilderment, I tried not to cringe.

"First," she began, "every get-high makes you depressed. Sure, you got high, but when you came down, the down was always lower than where you began. In time, your mood sinks lower and lower until you hit the deepest melancholy. Almost everyone who walks through the doors into rehab is clinically depressed. Fortunately, most of that clears with time."

"Second, everything you used to get wasted—pills, pot, coke, crack, smack, you name it—they're all brain poisons. They kill some neurons and make others deathly sick. By the time you reach these doors, your brain is one sick puppy. This toxicity can last for years."

Mike leaned over and whispered in my ear, "You are *still* toxic."

"Finally, and this is the big one, is the insanity of addiction itself. While the depression and toxicity will fade with time, this insanity is hardwired into your brain. It'll never go away."

I was sure she was looking straight at me.

"No matter that I have been clean and sober for years, no matter that I have worked the Steps and go to meetings regularly, no, this bit of twisted thinking will always be there. At the most unexpected moment, unbidden, and usually when I am at my weakest, the thought of using will come upon me. Hopefully, the spiritual tools I have learned in recovery will hold me in good stead."

"But this insane feeling can overpower all my good intentions. No matter that I know in my heart that I can never again drink or use like normal people do, the simple truth is that nothing I can do, indeed, no human power can do, will suffice to put down this craving. This is the moment when all my recovery work must be solid. I must have found access to a Higher Power. Only then can I pray my way out of my own perfect madness."

Denial

The room was packed as we sat listening to Abe G. talk about denial.

"Denial is a normal defense mechanism," he said, sipping his coffee. "For most people, it's a useful way to deal with the pain of reality, when that reality becomes too much to bear. A patient dying of lung cancer may know he's terminal, but he still must get up, shower and shave, and go out and meet the day. Denial buffers painful truth enough to allow us to function."

"But for us alcoholics and addicts of the world, denial becomes an essential tool to keep the madness of our addiction hidden from ourselves. We use denial to shield ourselves from the terrible truth of our disease, of what it's doing to our bodies, our minds, and our families. Denial builds an impenetrable wall of lies that prevents us from recognizing our powerlessness. It helps us turn a blind eye on the consequences of our using."

"You may hear your denial in these words. 'I don't have a problem—you have the problem.' 'No, I didn't forget where I parked my car. I'm sure I'll remember in a minute.' 'I don't need to drink, I just like to drink.' 'Sure, I drink Scotch every day, but you drink iced tea every day. What's the difference?' 'Yeah, I drink a lot, but not all that much really. Certainly not as much as my brother.' 'If you had my wife, you'd drink, too.' 'He arrested me for a DUI, but honestly, I only had two beers.' 'Yeah, I have a drinking problem, but it doesn't hurt anybody but me.' 'I know I have a problem with booze, but so did my mom and she lived to be ninety-six.' 'Sure, I'm an alcoholic, but I'm going to quit tomorrow.'"

"To begin the road that leads to recovery, the grip of denial must be broken. And it can only be broken by honesty."

As I listened, I made a mental list of Abe's signs of denial. I had them all, each and every one, but I refused to believe that I had any semblance of denial operating in me. No denial here.

Racing thoughts

Following our last session of the day, I had taken possession of the couch in our apartment for my afternoon nap. I was sleeping soundly when Mike dumped me off the couch and onto the floor.

"C'mon," he said. "You overslept. We're on our way to a meeting. You missed dinner—grab some chili off the stove and let's go."

I grumbled but found my shoes and stumbled to the kitchen. Mike ladled out a bowl of chili and plopped a thick slice of buttered bread on top.

"Thanks," I said. Shortly, I found myself in the back of John's Jeep heading down the Atlanta freeway, juggling my dinner in my lap.

The meeting hadn't begun by the time we arrived, so Mike and I stood outside on the porch, staring at the freeway overpass that filled the horizon. The traffic sped by on the highway like race cars at near light speed, taillights and headlights whizzing by in the hot Atlanta night.

"My thoughts race sometimes," said Mike. "They whir round and round in a high-speed dream. If most people's brain runs at 60 mph, then mine runs at 90. A slight tap on the peddle and I hit 120."

"Yeah," I said. "I know what you mean. Some nights, my thoughts keep me up all night. I keep going over and over what happened that day. Stupid stuff, mostly. Stuff I can't do anything about, but they can keep me awake all night."

"Sometimes I wake up in the night," said Mike, "worrying about the dumbest things and can never get back to sleep. By morning, I'm exhausted."

"I'm bipolar," I said. "Manic-depressive. I've been on meds for a long time, so racing thoughts are nothing new to me."

Mike turned to look at me in the evening light. "I suspect that I drank to quiet my mind."

"I'm sure of it," I said. "I know cocaine speeds most people up, but I think that for me, it actually slowed me down."

"Or at least allowed you to focus," said Mike. "Sam, my counselor, says mental illness is common in us drunks and junkies. And vice versa, people with some form of mental illness are far more likely to have trouble with drugs and alcohol."

"When my drinking got really bad," I said, "I quit taking all my meds. I'm pretty sure that made everything worse, but to be honest, at that point I just didn't care."

"Sam says using only makes my mental illness worse," he said.

In the growing darkness, I nodded.

Dual diagnosis

Today was my first encounter with Jane, the most feared of the counselors. She had a reputation as a tough-minded recovery Nazi. Mike had warned me to keep my head down. She was an imposing figure of a woman, tall and big-boned. Her henna-dyed hair was tied back in a bun, usually with a pencil sticking out. She tolerated no cross talk or silliness. She reminded me of my high school Latin teacher.

"Good morning, class," she intoned. "Who has a topic for today?"

The room fell mysteriously silent.

Jane crossed her arms over her chest and leaned back against her desk. She sucked air between her teeth and looked around the room, her gaze settling on me. I tried to become invisible but to no avail.

"You, mister, do you know what dual diagnosis is?"

"Uh…"

Mike rescued me. "Isn't that when we have some form of mental illness in addition to our addiction?"

She took her gaze off me and I breathed a sigh of relief.

"Yes," she said. "According to the National Survey on Drug Use and Health, almost half of people with addiction have a co-existing mental illness. And people diagnosed with a mental health condition are twice as likely to suffer from a substance use disorder. They go hand in hand."

She turned back to glare at me. "Why is this important?"

"Uh…"

Robert spoke up. "If we don't treat our psychiatric problem, we won't be able to stay sober."

"Precisely," said Jane, still staring at me. "What about you, numbskull? I hear you're batshit crazy."

"Uh," I said. "My shrink thinks I may be bipolar."

"Manic depression," said Jane. "Did you self-medicate? Did your cocaine slow you down?" She held a ruler in her right hand, ready to pop me if I misspoke. Mike had warned me about her tactics. "Who else?"

"I've got depression," said Robert.

"Borderline personality disorder," said Vera from the back of the room. "But I can't see how that's much different from being bipolar."

"Good point," said Jane, smiling beneficently at Vera.

"Over sixty percent of those people end up using drugs and alcohol."

"Attention-deficit hyperactive disorder," said Mike. "And obsessive-compulsive disorder."

"Let's not forget eating disorders and post-traumatic stress syndrome," said Jane. "Some would include generalized anxiety disorder, too."

"What about….?" I asked.

"Yes, Mr. Numbskull," said Jane, drawing near with her ruler poised to strike. "What happens if one of you crazies uses?"

"If we use, our mental illness gets worse," I said. "If we don't treat our particular form of insanity, we'll relapse," I said, gaining courage.

"And?"

"The old idea that recovery must proceed without the use of other drugs doesn't apply here," I said. "I must take the meds prescribed for my bipolar disease, or I will relapse."

"And?"

"And if I use again, I will die," I said.

Jane, lowering her ruler, actually smiled.

Depression hurts

Vera and I were at Fulton County Detox. It was her turn to lead the discussion and she was trying to lecture about the warning signs of relapse, but the clients were having none of it.

"I hurt," said Old Lady Olson, whose pleasure was to tipple Manischewitz from a crystal stem glass that was as old as she was. Mostly she sat alone drinking in the dark until one day her nephew dragged her to detox. "I hurt," she said again, pointing to her heart. "And I think I'm depressed."

"I knows I'm depressed," said Lula Mae, a heroin lady from uptown. "And I hurts, too, but mine is right here," she said, pointing at her stomach.

Even Old Man Fisher, who had spoken only six words since being admitted, shook off his torpor and spoke. "I don't know which came first, the depression or the drinking. But I do know one thing. Drink took the pain away."

Vera left the blackboard and stood next to Old Man Fisher.

"Where was your pain?" she asked.

Old Man Fisher pointed to his right temple and fell silent.

As the conversation moved around the circle, everyone admitted to depression linked to pain: two in the head, six in the chest, and four in the belly. All described the pain as sharp and all agreed with Mrs. Olson.

"I tried everything from aspirin to Goody powders to BCs," she said, "but nothing worked. Nothing but the booze. And the booze worked every time."

On the way home, Vera was silent for several minutes before she spoke.

"This is all very strange," she said.

"What?" I asked.

"All those people had painful depression that was relieved by alcohol." Vera turned to look at me. "I thought that only happened to me."

"And what medication, pray tell, did you prescribe for your pain, physician?"

"Vodka," she said, "straight up."

Alcoholic Insanity

Many factors contribute to the insanity of addiction.

The insanity of craving is hard-wired into our brains and will never leave us.

All get-highs are neurotoxins and poison the brain.

A hundred forms of negativity come to dominate our thinking.

My brain filters or ignores anything which would interfere with my using.

Depression is the result of long-term drug use.

Denial of our disease and its effects on others keeps us using.

Many mental illnesses are associated with addiction including bipolar disease, depression, obsessive-compulsive disorder, and PTSD.

Addictive Character Traits

> *"The fury of a demon instantly possessed me. I knew myself no longer. My original soul seemed, at once, to take its flight from my body; and a more than fiendish malevolence, gin-nurtured, thrilled every fibre of my frame."*
> —Edgar Allan Poe

I've seen it before

Dr. Taylor was leading a group discussion in one of the small classrooms. The white-haired gentleman looked especially professorial in his tweed jacket with leather elbow patches, smoking his pipe.

"My friends in psychiatry don't recognize the existence of an alcoholic personality type. I understand their reluctance to do so, but in my years in addiction medicine, I've seen the same character traits too many times to ignore them. I've observed that the traits of the addict at his worst were already present long before he began to drink."

Low self-esteem

"For types like us," said Robert; "it all begins with low self-esteem. Even as a kid, I always felt less than, if you know what I mean." We were walking from the apartments to a nearby high school stadium where we would run laps and exercise in the cool morning air before the sessions began at rehab. He and I, tubby as we were, must have looked a sight, trying to jog off twenty years of desk-sitting. Robert sat down on the bleachers and began lacing up his running shoes.

I thought for a minute then said, "I'm not sure I do."

"I was never good enough," said Robert. He began his stretching exercises. I pretended to know what I was doing and copied him. "No matter how hard I tried, I just didn't measure up. I didn't fit in. I always felt different, unwanted, on the outside looking in." He looked at me oddly as he straightened up. "I don't understand it, but I've always felt this way," he said.

As we stumbled around the track, I thought about what Robert had said, but it didn't ring true. I caught up with him at the water fountain.

"Most of us had a pretty normal upbringing," he said, panting. He took a long sip of water and straightened up. "Yet we all struggle with the idea that we're undeserving. Deep inside is the fear that no matter how hard we try, we'll never make the mark."

From somewhere deep in my mind came the memory of feeling very small and helpless. I was maybe three years old, trying to cross the road to a friend's house but I was frightened by the cars whizzing by. All alone, staring at the traffic, the world seemed monstrously huge and I was so very small and so very afraid.

"Maybe I'm frightened of a world that's spinning wildly out of control," said Robert.

Another memory leaped up, the day Mom took me to register for first grade. We walked into the school cafeteria and all I could see were monstrous stainless-steel pots and pans, giant mixers, and other ominous shining devices. I knew this had to be some terrible place, like the dentist's office. Something bad was surely about to happen and I clutched at my mother's hand. Panic, confusion, and bewilderment swept over me like a tide. School must be a horrible, horrible place. I began to cry. Why would my mother bring me here? Had I done something wrong? Confused and panicked, I had run crying from the cafeteria.

We walked silently back to the apartments, our towels posed stylishly over our shoulders. We had managed to round the track only once.

"At six years old, I was socially inept," Robert said. "It never got much better, not in high school, certainly not in college. I think the problem is that I'm too sensitive," he said.

I realized I had been lost in thought and had missed what he was saying.

"What?" I asked.

Overly sensitive hearts

"Our hearts are too big, too easily hurt," he said. "We simply feel too deeply. Despite the lies we told when we were deep in our addiction, we're basically honest people, honest to a fault. But we can't stand the dishonesty and hypocrisy we see all around us. We can't stand the pain of the world. As a result, we shut down our hearts. We refuse to feel the pain."

My head was reeling. This was too much to grasp all at once.

"For most people, the head and the heart are in balance, working to achieve some kind of mental equilibrium, so to speak," he said. "Normally, the heart is the source of our emotions, our conscience, and our creativity. The ego's best suited for calculating, measuring things. Its strong suit is logic, and it loves to be in control. By shutting down our feelings, we give the ego full rein. Uncontrolled by the heart, its influence grows out of proportion and it wants to rule the world. Hell, mine thinks it *is* God."

"The ego-maniac with an inferiority complex!" I said.

"We become arrogant, judgmental, cock-sure of our own self-importance."

"But it's all a game to hide the low self-esteem," I said. It was starting to make sense.

Wearing the mask

Rummaging in his closet, Timmy found a bag full of streamers and a zombie Halloween mask.

"It belonged to Merle," I said.

Timmy put the mask on and stomped around the room in his best monster imitation. He paraded into the living room where Mike and I were on the couch.

"Need eat brains! NOW!" bellowed Timmy.

"Get outa here witch yo' bad self," said Mike, grinning.

"Oooh!" I said. "I love masks. Let me wear it."

"You should," said Mike. "All good addicts and alcoholics wear a mask every day."

"How's that?" I asked.

"I wore a mask to hide my low self-esteem," said Mike. "I hid because I was afraid that if you really knew who I was you wouldn't like me."

Robert walked in munching a candy bar and plopped down on the couch. "We think we're fooling everybody," he said, "but in truth, everybody knows we're drunks and junkies, and we're only fooling ourselves."

"I think I know what you mean," said Timmy. "I was sure I was fooling everybody at the pharmacy, but in the end, they were the ones who called the Pharmacy Board. They knew all along."

"I used my mask to look good in front of others," Robert admitted. "I invented a whole persona just to impress you and keep my true self hidden."

"I know I spent a lot of effort trying to please everybody," said Timmy. "I wanted to look good. I even went to my wife's hairdresser and got my hair styled. I got myself elected as a delegate to the Iowa Pharmacy Convention just so I could admire myself in the mirror."

"Poor little Timmy Pharma-man," teased Robert swallowing the last of the candy bar and licking his fingers. "Nobody loves him."

Controlling behavior

Robert was knocking on the apartment door. My roommates had already left for the center, and he was in a hurry to find breakfast.

"Hurry up," he called, pounding, "or we won't have time to eat before morning spiritual."

Out the door and walking to rehab, I asked Robert, "You said something about controlling behavior? What makes you think I have it?"

Robert laughed. He giggled and jiggled as he avoided the ruts in the path.

"First off, you need to remember what I told you yesterday," he said, appearing half-serious for a moment.

"Uh," I said, not wishing to admit I had forgotten.

"If you spot it, you got it," he said.

"Oh, yeah," I remembered. "When I see a character defect in another person it's because I have it myself. If I criticize someone about their behavior, it's because I recognize that behavior in myself."

"Because I'm a controlling SOB.," he said, "I can spot controlling behavior in you, you controlling SOB."

We laughed. I just managed to avoid a large tree root in the path.

"So, what is it?" I asked. "Controlling behavior, I mean?"

"Because of my inferiority complex, I live in terror of what the world and the people in it are going to do to me. Like, you know, steal my woman, invade my country, make me look bad in front of the boss. Makes my thoughts spin out of control. The inside of my head becomes a very dangerous place."

"Ouch," I said, embarrassed at his description of myself.

"So, I do my very best to control everything outside in the mistaken belief that if I can, I can control the chaos inside."

"Sounds reasonable to me," I quipped.

"Not!" said Robert. "The more I persist in trying to control the world, the more uncomfortable I get, because in reality I'm powerless over this thing called life."

"So, I can never win the game called me-in-control-of-the-world, eh?"

"Absolutely not. It also explains my overwhelming need to be in charge," said Robert. "By being successful—and powerful—I think I can control the events in my life." He stopped outside the cafeteria and leaned against the wall. breathing heavily.

"And the less deserving I feel, the lower my self-esteem," I said glumly. "Then my ego compensates by inflating my self-importance even more. And the more arrogant and judgmental I become."

"Right," he said. "I have to be better than everybody else, and I always have to be right." He reached over and poked me in the chest. "And my opinion is the only correct one and I don't mind telling you so. But let's forget that for now," said Robert as we entered the cafeteria. "It's breakfast!" He grabbed a tray. "Let's eat."

Breakfast was one of Robert's three favorite meals. I laughed and followed him.

Emotional clamp

We were hanging out in the break room when the sound of feet running up and down the hall filled the air, followed by the sound of more feet and yelling, then the yelling became louder and more insistent.

"Where's the fire extinguisher?" said the first voice.

Then a second voice, "Somebody hit the alarm!"

And finally, "FIRE!"

We were out of our seats and running for the exit. Outside we huddled up in the parking lot. People poured from every exit until almost a hundred of us were milling around outside. Bright yellow fire engines arrived, and figures in yellow suits with oxygen tanks on their backs hurried into the building. There was no smoke, no sign of flames.

"Where's the fire?" asked Bill, the new guy in our apartment.

Bill was an anesthesiologist from Augusta who didn't think he had a problem but was in rehab just to be sure, he said.

"Don't know yet," I said. In a few minutes, we learned that the fire was in a wastebasket in Administration.

"I'll bet that Jerry dumped his pipe in the trash can again," said Robert. "Hey, isn't it time for lunch?" The cafeteria was in the next building over, the one without the fire trucks. "C'mon," he said. "Let's go eat."

The specialty of the day was baked chicken. Robert examined the chicken on his plate as if it were a specimen to be dissected.

"Chicken flambeau, I suspect," he said. "Must be a refugee from the fire sale next door." He turned the chicken over with his fork. "Fire sale, heavily discounted goods. Sounds like us—heavily discounted goods. All with substantially lowered value."

We laughed. "Fire Sale" was the nickname given to the Tuesday afternoon session that everyone attended, not just physicians and nurses but the nonmedical types as well: lawyers, dentists, and business people, anybody with enough money to cover the cost of country club rehab. And today was Tuesday.

After lunch, we assembled in the large hall next to the cafeteria. The rehab founder, Dr. Taylor, had dragged himself down from the ivory tower to address the multitudes.

"Good afternoon," he said in glowing tones. "Today, I would like us to discuss the issues of the heart. Why do we live in our heads? Why do we shut down our feelings? And why should we change?"

"Uh-oh," said Robert, digging me in the ribs with his elbow.

"Who will start?" asked Dr. Taylor.

The room was quiet for a long moment until Timmy spoke.

"I don't understand," he said. "Of course, I live in my head. Where else would I be? And I have feelings just like everyone else. I don't understand."

"Robert," said Dr. Taylor, "would you care to enlighten Timmy?"

"Told ya so," whispered Robert under his breath. In full voice, he said, "Yes, sir. I don't know about Timmy, but for me, growing up, I found that my feelings just tore me up. They hurt so much I learned to shut them down."

Suddenly I remembered the emotional pain I felt as a teenager, when suddenly my wonderful family life was smashed by events unforeseen and out of control. I raised my hand.

"When I was fifteen, my brother died of leukemia," I said. "He'd been sick for less than a year and he died just before Christmas. I can remember feeling like my heart had been torn apart, like giant hands ripping a phone book apart." I paused for breath and to let my heart rate slow.

"Then just as suddenly, almost exactly a year later, my father died of a heart attack," I said. "I remember thinking, Well, I've done this before, and I know what this funeral stuff is all about. I know what to do. But the experience wasn't like before. I felt numb all over. It was as if a giant emotional clamp had come down over my heart and shut down all my feelings. Somewhere deep inside me, a voice said, Enough. You've had enough pain. You won't feel anything now. You must be protected! Ever since, that clamp has been with me, shutting down any emotion that threatened to upset me. Has anyone else experienced anything like this? Or am I just nuts?"

"I'm sure you're more than a little crazy," said Dr. Taylor, "but let's see who else has a similar experience. A show of hands, please."

Hands went up from over two-thirds of the audience. I was shocked.

Self-centered

"When did I become so self-centered?" asked Timmy. We were sitting at the kitchen table in the apartment while he worked on his moral inventory, writing down all the bad things he had done so he could see the character defects that shaped them.

"I've made this list of my mistakes," he said, "and figured out which of my character defects led to each one. For example, I lied about stealing Ritalin so no one would discover my using. I was afraid I'd lose my license or worse. In other words, I was afraid of losing something I had, which led to my dishonesty."

"Sounds good," I said. "Go on."

"But each example points to selfishness on my part—every one," Timmy said. "Dishonest sometimes. Lazy sometimes. Sometimes afraid, but always self-centered." He shook his head. "I never thought of myself that way before. Timmy is a very selfish person."

I picked up the Big Book and read, "Selfishness, self-centeredness! That, we think, is the root of our troubles."

Timmy hung his head with his hands covering his ears. "Oh, my aching ego," he said.

Above the rules

We were in Jane's class. I was late and had to sit in front. My tardiness did not go unnoticed.

"Self-aggrandizement," said Jane, ruler in hand, ready to rap the knuckles of anyone who offended. "Who can tell me about self-aggrandizement?"

Robert leaned over and whispered to me.

"Best get the torture over with quickly," he said. Then aloud, "Self-aggrandizement is when I falsely exaggerate my own self-importance. But what I'm really doing is hiding my low self-esteem."

"You are a dirty little boy, you are," said the unflappable Jane, "but out of our infinite kindness we shall permit you to live another day."

"Blessings be unto the compassionate Jane," Robert quipped.

Still striding the room, Jane said, "And how does the self-important person act, pray tell?"

"Self-importantly?" I asked, the words leaping unbidden from my foolish mouth. Jane was headed for me, ruler raised, when Mike spoke.

"He comes to believe in his own importance," said Mike. "He's better than everyone else, and he doesn't mind telling you so."

"Go on," said Jane, her gaze still fixed on me.

"One does find oneself somewhat above the rules," John said. "Why, I can recall once when Lin said, Rules were made for people who can't think for themselves."

Jane's ruler came down smartly on top of my head right where my bald spot is. I nearly said ouch but thought better of it.

"Explain yourself, Old Man," said Jane, standing over me.

"Well, when I was a young man," I began, "my mother told me, think for yourself."

"Good advice," she said. "A wise woman, I'm sure."

"But," I continued, "being a good alcoholic, I translated that into 'Rules are made for people who can't think for themselves'. By virtue of my advanced brain, I was entitled to make up my own rules. Being a person of superior intelligence, I didn't have to follow the rules that lesser people did."

"I suppose you used your superior intelligence to tell other people what they needed to do?" asked Jane.

"Well, I certainly tried."

"And how did that work for you?" asked Jane.

"It got me here," I said, rubbing the top of my head.

King Baby

Jane had asked one of the women to bring in a picture of herself as a baby, and we passed it around. It seemed to me an unremarkable photo of a two-year-old who would grow up to be a family practitioner and a Demerol addict.

Jane held up the photo and asked, "What do you see?" After listening to the usual banal compliments, Jane shook her head. "Nope. What I see here is King Baby trying to control the adult person. King Baby is a way to think of our behavior as adult alcoholics and addicts. King Baby lives a fear-based life in where he is the most important person in the world. If he's wet, hungry, or cold, people come running to tend to his needs. He is the personification of dominating self-will. Such behavior is useful when we're in diapers, but not as an adult."

I looked again at the photo. This time I saw a young child whose eyes were filled with fear. She reached out to control everything in her world to avoid acknowledging her inadequacies.

My mother used to show me a picture of myself as a baby, sailor suit, curly ringlets under a sailor's cap. She always glowed at the image of her precious son, but today, for the first time, I recalled the image of a child fearful of a world he could not understand. My King Baby was terrified of everything.

Playing the victim

Leon, the rabbi from Cleveland, was holding forth at morning spiritual. He had his prayer shawl around his shoulders and his hands folded in prayer.

"Good morning to you all," he said, fidgeting nervously with a button on his sleeve. "My name's Leon. If I seem a trifle nervous today, it's because I feel like a lion about to be eaten by the Christians. Seriously, my buddy Jaime, who was here last year, said that as a Jew, this was a tough room to play. Jaime said that they'd try to turn me into a Christian. I'm beginning to understand that, though I don't see why Moses couldn't run a good rehab."

"Today," he said, "I'm going to share one of my deepest dark secrets. They say that if you tell on your disease, it loses power over you. So, I'm going to tell on myself and maybe I'll get better. My secret—hold onto your hats—my secret is that I like to play the martyr. Imagine that."

The room busted out laughing.

"No matter what happened," he said, "I was always the victim. Nothing was ever my fault. But that always put me in a bad place, so I drank. First, a little Manischewitz with dinner, then some with lunch. Eventually, I moved up to Napa Valley wines. I can't remember when I went from being a social drinker to a real souse. By the way, did you hear the one about the alcoholic who only drank with the crowd? Said he was a 'social' drinker. If anybody was having a drink, he said, so shall I. Get it? So shall I?"

I kept waiting for the shepherd's crook to come out, but it never did.

"Okay," he said, grinning. "I hope you enjoyed the show. I'll be appearing nightly at the local AA meeting house and be sure to bring your yarmulke. But we won't be serving any wine."

I am happy to say he received a standing ovation for his efforts.

Unreasonable expectations

The next day, we met with Jane again.

"Good morning, class," she said. "Who has a topic for this morning?"

The room fell oddly silent, again.

I raised my hand. "We were talking about the character faults of the alcoholic and addict earlier in Matt's session."

"I try not to come into conflict with Matt," she said, "but let's venture into the void, shall we? As a recovering alcoholic myself, I have a tendency toward unreasonable expectations. Anyone have a similar experience?"

"I do sometimes let my expectations get overblown," I said.

"High expectations, low serenity," she quoted the common axiom. "Low expectations, high serenity."

"I can almost live on high expectations," said Vera, sitting near the front of the room. "I feed the yearning in my heart on them. Surely something glorious will happen tomorrow that will change my life for the better. Happiness is certainly just around the next corner."

"Tomorrow something wonderful will happen that will solve all my problems, right?" asked Jane.

"I constantly dream of winning the lottery," said Mike.

"So, you buy a lottery ticket every day," she said, "even though you know the odds are millions to one."

"Yes, but those odds don't apply to me," said Mike. "I'm above the rules that ordinary people have to follow. I am the Lord of the Long Shots."

Timid Timmy raised his hand.

"I had an alcoholic uncle who lived on pipe dreams," he said.

"You do know what a pipe dream is, don't you?" she asked.

Robert, who liked poetry, spoke up. "The poet Coleridge used to smoke opium until he passed out. When he woke up, he would turn his drugged pipe dreams into poetry," he said.

"Go on," Jane said to Timmy.

"Anyway," he said, "Uncle Paul was always spinning elaborate get-rich schemes that were going to make him wealthy. Once he wanted me to invest in an exhausted silver mine. He said there was still enough silver left to generate a few thousand a month, and what with the price of silver going up—well, you get it. Another time he cooked up a scheme to invest in used-up oil wells in Texas, same idea."

"Sounds like me," said Mike. "I always jump into everything whole hog. If it's worth doing, it's worth doing to excess."

"Yes, but these wild schemes never work, and I'm always left empty-handed," said Robert.

"High expectations, low serenity," repeated Timmy. "Yes, I know that one."

Jane almost twinkled.

Overthinking

Jane was pacing back and forth at the front of the room. She was in her element.

"I'm having trouble figuring this out," said Timmy.

"Quit trying to analyze everything," said Jane. "Some things cannot be understood by the mind. They have to be felt. Mike?"

"Not only do I try to analyze everything," said Mike, "I overanalyze everything. My mind can spin itself into some unbelievable places. I can make mountains out of molehills faster than you can say Mount Everest."

Reggie spoke next. "I remember coming home early one Spring day. My wife wasn't there, which seemed unusual for that time of day. I wandered into the bedroom and found a matchbook from the Oasis Bar on her dresser. My God, I thought, that place is a meat market; people show up there to get laid. What's she doing there? Then I remembered how distant she seemed lately. We haven't had sex in almost a month. Oh, shit, I thought, she's meeting someone at that bar. She's having an affair! I knew it! Well, that does it. We're getting a divorce! She can have the house, but I'm keeping the boat. And *she* has to take that goddamn cat! Then I opened the matchbook cover. Inside it read, 'Julia, the newcomer Alice needs a sponsor really badly. Could you call her at home?' I was so embarrassed that my cheeks turned red. My overthinking had taken me to the brink of insanity in under thirty seconds."

After a long pause, Jane spoke. "You must learn to listen with your heart," she said, coming to a stop in front of me. "Analysis is the province of the mind, not the heart. Let yourself feel! Quit trying to analyze everything. It only gets you into trouble."

I started to say something but thought better of it. Good move.

We beat ourselves up

Lunch tray in hand, I sat down between Robert and Timmy. Mike had arrived earlier and was sitting across from me, sipping his coffee.

"Good morning, gentlemen," I said.

"Timmy," said Robert, munching on his salad, "are you still being too hard on yourself?'

Timmy blushed but said nothing.

"We are hard on ourselves," said Mike. "I'm my own worst critic."

"I'm certainly an expert at putting myself down," said Robert. "In fact, I invented my own personal Ass-Kicking-Machine. Just drop a quarter in the slot, bend over, and get a royal ass-kicking."

Timmy laughed. "You're right," he said. "I remember the day I graduated from pharmacy school. I felt that somehow the whole graduation process was a sham."

"Did you cheat on your final exams?" asked Robert.

"No! But I felt like I didn't deserve the honor. I just knew someday the big people would discover I was a fraud and come and take my license away."

"The big people may come and do just that," said Mike.

There was a momentary pause as embarrassed forks filled mouths.

"One of the best ways you can tell if someone's finally getting into recovery," said Mike between sips of coffee, "is they learn to take a compliment. If you try to compliment a newcomer, they just shrug it off—they know they're undeserving."

"Isn't there a poem about banging your head against the wall until it comes back bloody, beaten, and bowed?" asked Timmy. "Seems my head is always bloody."

"'Under the bludgeoning of chance, my head is bloody, but unbowed, that Invictus thing,'" said Robert. He continued, 'I am the master of my fate, I am the captain of my soul.'"

"Well, my head is definitely beaten up," said Mike. "For most of my medical career, I felt undeserving of the respect and the income I received. I couldn't enjoy life. I was always waiting for the other shoe to fall."

"I know what you mean," said Timmy, his head down.

Enabling

"Enabling," said Matt leaning back against the table and sipping his coffee. "In the days of my using, I was adept at manipulating others so they would support my using. Or at least, not slow me down. What about you, Timmy?"

"I would lie to my wife so I could go to the pharmacy at night and get high at and screw the saleslady."

"That's good, I guess," said Matt. "What did you tell her?"

"Uh…" began Timmy.

"That he had an itch that needed scratching!" Mike interjected.

Laughter filled the room. Timmy blushed. "I told her that I needed to go work on the books, or that the auditor was coming, whatever I could think of," he said. "She never questioned anything I said, never complained."

"My kind of woman!" said Mike.

"Hush, Mike," said Matt. "Leon?"

Leon spoke next. "I used to come home drunk at 3 am every morning, park the car in the garage, then fall asleep in it," said Leon. "Dutifully, my wife would get out of bed, haul me inside, and tuck me into bed. Did it every night, at least until her counselor told her she was enabling me."

"What did she do then?" asked Matt.

"She let me sleep in the car," said Leon.

A voice from the front of the room spoke. "One time I got drunk, took my pistol out to the country club, and shot up all the ducks in the pond. All anyone ever said was, 'Good shooting, doc.'"

"We make other people dependent on us," said Matt, "or do the opposite, allow ourselves to be dependent on someone else."

"I never did that," I said, to a chorus of boos.

The hole in my chest

Matt led the first session of the next day. The morning light coming through the windows of the classroom was soft and serene, so I took a seat up front near the window. It was show-and-tell day.

"What do you know about the character of a person who's addicted to drugs or alcohol?" asked Matt. His blue eyes were clear and sharp, as if looking into our deepest natures.

"It's bad!" yelled someone from the back of the room.

"Wrong answer," said Matt. "Try again."

"I have a hole in my chest I can't fill," said Vera, sitting across from me.

"That's a good start," he said. "Are you drunks and junkies uncomfortable in your own skin?"

A chorus of hoots and hollers erupted in the room.

"What does it mean, I have a hole in my chest?" asked Matt. "Robert?"

"For some reason," Robert began, "I have a yearning, gnawing feeling, a craving if you will, that's always there. I've never felt truly comfortable in any situation. Always out of place, irritable, or edgy."

"Restless, irritable, and discontent!" came the same voice from the back of the room. I would have said the voice was Mike's, but he was sitting next to me.

"Good," said Matt. "Go on."

"Then I discovered marijuana," said Robert, grinning. A few tokes and I felt great. I could relax at last. I could talk to girls. I was finally at peace with myself."

"Then what happened?" asked Matt.

"Pot led to snorting cocaine, which led to crack," said Robert. "Then the roof fell in."

"Did it hurt?" asked Mike.

"It still hurts," said Robert.

"What about you, preacher," he said, looking at Reggie.

"With me it was alcohol," said my friend. "As my discomfort got worse, I found that a mixed drink at dinner really took the edge off. I called it Attitude Adjustment Hour."

"What happened then?" asked Matt with his avuncular smile.

"One drink led imperceptibly to two," said Reggie. "Before I realized what was happening, my using had grown to a bottle every night. Every time I went out, I carried a flask of whiskey with me."

"So, we have a hunger, an aching in our chest quenched only by booze or drugs," said Matt.

He turned and stared at me.

"I found that other things could fill the hole, but only for a while," I said. "Like buying an expensive new car so I could impress the ladies."

"And ...?" asked Matt.

"At first," I said, "women filled the front seat and the world noticed how cool I was. Then, the women left for a faster car, the first car payment came due, and someone keyed the hood of the car."

"You lost your buzz, didn't you?" he asked.

"Yep."

Vera was next.

"My parents used to make beer in the basement, and they would let me sip some now and then, but frankly the taste of it made me sick," she said. "And I never could stand the aroma of whiskey or how it made me feel the next day, so I was never much of a drinker, not even in college. I did smoke some pot, but in med school I just didn't have time for fooling around."

"When I joined the faculty, I would attend recruiting dinners where potential new professors were being wined and dined. The wine gave me a buzz that reminded me of pot. I found I enjoyed the yeasty aroma and I never got a hangover. Fine wine was certainly part of the good life I had worked so hard to earn. In time, I would only eat lunch at restaurants with a wine list. I had no idea how bad my boozing had gotten until the Department Chairman showed up one morning with a ticket to Atlanta."

Blanche was sitting up front and Matt called on her next.

"I'm thirty-seven and I'm from Alabama, the old South, don't you know?" said the petite Southern Belle. "I started on mint juleps when I was sixteen, all the debs did, don't you know? In my sorority at Ole Miss drinking was the *in* thing and of course I went along, I mean, doesn't everyone drink at parties and whenever a young lady needs to soothe her spirits just a bit. And I've been drinking a little since, which is really the polite thing to do in the best social circles don't you know, but really not that much really. And I heard that a little wine is good for your heart, all you doctors know that. My children made me come here. I'm sure when I dry out a bit, everything will be just fine. Have you heard about how good the new wines from Australia are this year?"

Matt stared sadly at Blanche but said nothing. Then he turned to Dolores, an attractive woman sitting in the back. She looked lost. Like Blanche, Dolores was a newcomer, a nurse married to a physician who had dumped her at the door to rehab and left. She was addicted to heroin and had run through over $100,000 of her husband's money before he got his credit cards back. Now, he wanted none of her.

"What did you use to fill the hole in your chest, Dolores?" he asked.

"Pain pills, at first," she said. "Soon I was stealing morphine from the narcotics cabinet at work and after I got fired I took to buying heroin off the street. When I ran out of money I would screw for dope. I screwed a lot of guys and did a lot of smack."

"How's that going for you?" asked Matt.

"I've lost fifty pounds, I have tracks up and down my arms, my nursing license is gone, and my husband has disowned me."

"What else?"

"I'm HIV positive."

Addictive Character Traits

Addicts share certain characteristics that feed
into our addiction.

Low self-esteem, driven by fear, is the most important.

The hearts of addicts are overly sensitive.
We feel the pain of the world intensely.

We shut down the heart to avoid the pain
which gives the ego full rein.

The ego, driven by fear, wants to control the world.

We wear an emotional mask to hide from the
world.

Over time, self-centeredness and arrogance
dominate our thinking. We are above the rules.

Our expectations become out of sync with
reality, resulting in resentments and anger.

We over-analyze everything, making mountains
out of molehills.

Begin with Baby Steps

"Take the first step in faith.
You don't have to see the whole staircase,
just take the first step."
—Martin Luther King, Jr.

Ego deflation

Jane had me by the throat during group session. Her flaming red hair perfectly complemented the flaming red of her cheeks. She seemed determined to nail my hide to the wall.

"I guess you think you're a pretty smart guy, huh?" she asked me.

"Yes, I think so," I said warily.

"You're so smart you woke up one morning and decided to become a drunk and a junkie, right?"

"Well, no, not exactly."

"But it was your very best thinking that got you here, right?"

"Yes, but ..." I knew she had me.

"I understand you almost died, is that right?" she asked.

"I guess so. Yeah, that's right."

"So, your over-inflated ego almost got you killed?"

"If you say so." Instant regret.

"Listen, mister, if you don't lose that ego of yours, you'll use again, and if you use again, you'll die."

I didn't like the sound of that, but I knew it was true. For me, to use again would be to die.

"You ever been to boot camp, boy?" Jane asked with a razor-sharp edge to her voice.

"No, sir," I felt like saluting.

"In boot camp, they take away your fancy clothes, shave your head, and teach you to march in formation just like everybody else. Your hot-shot personality will be of no use to you when the enemy starts shooting. If I'm your drill instructor, my job is to give you the skills you need to stay alive when the battle starts. Right, boy?"

"Yes, sir!" I really wanted to salute.

"If a dumb plebe thinks he knows more than his sergeant, he'll get us all killed, won't he?"

"Right, sir, yes, sir." This time I did salute.

"This isn't funny, dumbass!" she screamed. "If you fuck this up and go out again, you will die and it won't be pretty! Got that?"

"Yessir!"

"Then shut up and pay attention," she said. "And from today on, when you come in my room, you'd better check that ego of yours at the door."

The next morning in group, Matt took his turn at whacking down my ego. He was bearing down on me in all my ignorance.

"I hope you're hearing this," he growled at me. "You're no longer driving the bus. You're not even the navigator. From now on, you sit in the back just like everyone else. Maybe you can even learn to enjoy the ride. We're all just bozos on this bus, you most of all."

I blinked.

"I've been having trouble wrapping my head around that," I said.

"You still need to be taken down a few notches," he barked. "You are your biggest problem. That mind of yours is going to kill you. Not only that, but you need to understand that you're no better and no worse than any other human being. In a hundred years, no one will remember either one of us. Here, let me read this."

He took a book from his desk and read, "Blinded by my own brilliance, I could not fathom any other point of view but my own. But if I were to find my heart and the Higher Power that came with it, I had to abandon the idea that I was God and surrender the self-will that had all but destroyed me."

I was too embarrassed to respond.

"Get this," he said, "you'll use again, and if you use again …"

"I'll die," I said, the words echoing in my ears like a death knell.

Unconventional knowledge

I was willing to accept the fact that there might be more to the universe than what I could measure, more than what the Hubble telescope could see. I only hoped I wasn't opening the door to crystals, chakras, and séances. My first real taste of unconventional knowledge came one evening during a meeting in our apartment.

Alan was a tall rangy GP who had lost his license and his practice. He was at the end of his stay in rehab and when he shared, his words had the ring of truth.

We gathered in the apartment waiting on dinner, talking about the meaning of coincidence. I sat cross-legged on the floor with my back to the wall.

"Sometimes it seems I'm the beneficiary of a lot of happy coincidences," came a voice from the other side of the room.

Alan spoke. "One thing I've learned here," he said, "there are no coincidences. They are simply God's way of remaining anonymous."

As I leaned against the wall, I wasn't sure I could accept his words at face value. Then suddenly, out of nowhere, came the certainty of Alan's truth. It landed, not in my mind, but somewhere in my gut, well below the level of my conscious mind—the idea that coincidences were God's way of working behind the scenes. Without any effort on my part, I knew it was true. I hadn't looked up any references, searched the literature, taken a poll, or asked for a consensus. I simply knew it was true. New knowledge had entered into me, not through my mind but through my heart. Knowledge from unconventional sources.

Then Robert chimed in. "There's no such thing as luck, or chance," he said. "Nothing happens in God's world by mistake."

God's words in my ear

"Coming home from a meeting yesterday, I had a strange experience," I told Father Mick as we walked along.

The priest nodded.

"We were driving back to the center at sunset," I said. "The sky was awesome, shades of orange and pink. I felt almost, well, contented."

We paused as Father Mick lit his pipe.

"We were in the van and I was sitting by the window with Robert and Alan sitting beside me. John went around a corner a little too fast and both Robert and Alan slammed into me, shoving me against the window. In the same moment, words were driven into my head like the platen of an old manual typewriter being slammed across the page. What I heard was, 'God doesn't want you to drink, use drugs, or kill yourself'. The voice was my own, but it had more power and authority than any thought I've ever had."

Father Mick nodded as a curl of smoke encircled his head.

"I could understand the part about not drinking or using drugs," I said. "That's what my mind would have said. But the part about committing suicide was something I would never have thought of."

"Maybe the universe was reaching out to you," he said.

"That's what I thought," I said, "but I don't understand …"

"Don't try," said Father Mick, smiling. "Understanding is highly overrated."

Leaning into the flow

Leon and I were walking to morning spiritual. His step was lighter and his smile more sincere than in recent days.

"So now you'll tell me how to get rid of my selfishness and the rest of my character defects?" I asked.

"I'll try," he said.

We walked on in silence for a while.

"Imagine yourself floating down a sparkling blue river, with banks of the most luscious green foliage, the most brilliant blue sky, and the whitest of white clouds floating above. You're filled with peace. In this moment you have no fear, nothing to drive your character defects to the surface. When your defects were active, they protected you from the world, hid your addiction, and helped you gain advantage over others."

"But now, for this single moment, you have no need for any of them. In this moment, in the here and now and just for this moment, let's agree to do away with all your defects of character. Lust, greed, pride, all of them.

Let's hold to the faith that if you do this, everything will be all right. That whatever problems come up in the future, you won't have to resort to old thinking. Your new way of new thinking will protect you."

"You won't be able to hold onto this perfect moment for very long. Pretty soon the material world will begin knocking on the door of your mind, wanting in. But now, for one second, you know with absolute certainty that you no longer require any of your shortcomings. The process of reducing them to manageable levels will be long and slow, and you'll never be completely free of them, but never again will they control you. In this moment of clarity, ask God to remove them all."

"I'm gonna have to think about this," I said.

"Yes," he said, "you will."

Spiritual pride

I had a weekend pass and visited my cousin in the poor down-east part of Carolina. He's a recovering alcoholic and we talked and went to a meeting at his home group. Driving back, I took a slow and winding route through the lowliest parts of the hinterland. Pig farms, pickup trucks, and old weathered farmhouses lined the highway. When I returned to rehab, I spoke with Reggie about my experience.

"I had another experience of unconventional knowledge," I said. "My cousin and I spent a wonderful weekend just hanging out. I was in a very peaceful state of mind when I left."

"What's the punch line?" asked Reggie.

"As I drove through the lowlands, I noticed an endless array of small churches. The Brethren of Redemption, the Second National Church of God, Bought by the Blood, the True Church of Gospel Holiness, you know. Most were humble little buildings, some not much more than shanties. In the glow of my new-found spirituality I was sure I was now on the one true path. My spiritual arrogance made me superior to such lowly houses of worship. I asked myself, why are there so many of these insignificant little churches?"

"Did you get your comeuppance?" he laughed.

"A message as strong as steel and angry as a bull erupted inside my head."

"Yes?" said Reggie.

"'BECAUSE I LIKE THEM,' the voice resounded. 'BECAUSE I LIKE THEM.'"

Honesty

"H stands for honesty," said Robert as he and Mike and I piled into the car. It would be a long drive to an Old Timer's AA meeting on the other side of Atlanta.

"Honesty is the spiritual principle behind the first step of AA, right?" I said, taking the backseat while Robert slid into the driver's seat. As we drove out of the parking lot, we picked up Reggie, completing the foursome.

"Reggie," said Robert, "we're trying to explain to our buddy here the true meaning of honesty."

"The spiritual principle behind the first step," said Reggie.

"We got that part already," said Robert, turning and talking over his right shoulder.

"Eyes on the road," said Mike.

"How about this," said Reggie. "The honesty of the first step is the only part of recovery that has to be perfect."

"How's that?" I asked.

"If the house of your recovery is built on a shaky foundation," said Reggie, "everything that follows will collapse when you need it most. The first bit of honesty is this—I must accept in my heart and mind that I'm an alcoholic and an addict, and that will never change. That I'll never again be able to drink like a normal person. That my life, as I'd been living it, was simply not working. Until I do this, I can't accept the help that'll save my ass."

"Amen," said Reggie. "On your new journey, you're going to find some old virtues you had forgotten about, like charity, compassion, and kindness. But none will be perfect. However, if your honesty is perfect, everything that follows will turn out fine."

Robert craned his neck toward the back seat. "You have to be honest about your mistakes, too," he said.

"Eyes forward, please!" Mike said.

"You must learn to admit your mistakes," said Robert, "no matter how impossible that seems now."

Mike spoke up. "And honesty is more than just telling the truth," he said. "Your honesty will force you to look clearly at who and what you are. It's how you'll face yourself, your character defects, your fears."

"Honesty is a way of living, of doing things," shouted Robert over his shoulder. Suddenly the traffic on the freeway came to a complete stop. After looking both ways, Robert turned completely around in his seat. "If I'm walking across campus and throw a gum wrapper on the ground, I'm being dishonest. I can't ignore my responsibilities or my bad behavior any longer."

"When I hide my feelings," said Mike, "that's dishonesty, too."

"No more swallowing emotions," said Robert.

"Hiding behind your mask of superiority," said Reggie.

There was a merciful pause in the conversation as an ambulance flew by.

"As children of God, we're born with an honest heart," said Reggie. "We started out expecting, I don't know, something. But what we found was hypocrisy and mendacity. But we ended up dealing with the world's dishonesty by surrendering to it. We learned to deny the things that caused us pain. In time, we came to speak in half-truths. By the time we reached our bottom, lying was second nature."

"You know how you can tell if an alcoholic is lying?" asked Mike, grinning. Somehow, I knew his riddle was about to land on my head.

"Okay, I give," I said. "How can you tell if an alcoholic is lying?"

"Because his lips are moving!" said my three friends in unison. My face got hot. I knew it was crimson.

We were approaching the meeting house when Mike spoke again. "There are four ways you can tell when someone's starting to get recovery. First, they stop cursing."

"When you clean up your mind," said Robert, "your mouth will follow."

"Second, they quit driving like a madman," said Reggie. "They're no longer above the rules and now they obey the traffic laws." John's manic driving style immediately came to mind.

Mike again: "Third, they can finally accept a compliment, because they're learning their true worth as a human being.

"Last," said Robert, "they quit lying."

We pulled into the parking lot at the meeting house. I sat quietly for a moment, remembering what Matt had said, "Honesty is as addictive as anything else. But it's sweet and clean." I took a deep breath, let out a sigh, and walked into the meeting.

The conversation about honesty continued the next day in Jane's group.

"Honesty is the first spiritual principle, and perhaps the most important one," she said. "Why is that?"

"Because honesty is the lamp of Diogenes," said Timmy. "Without it, I can't find truth."

"What about dishonesty, Timmy?" she asked. "Tell me about that."

"Well, first is cash register dishonesty, where I steal the money from the cash drawer when nobody's looking." He paused for a moment and seemed lost when Robert jumped in.

"Emotional dishonesty. When I hide my emotions under a smokescreen," he said.

"Oh, yeah," said Timmy, "like, I'm fine, you're fine. We're all here in rehab because we're all so fine."

"But the worst are the lies we tell ourselves," said Reggie. "If I tell the same lie often enough, even I'll start to believe it. These are the hardest untruths to get shed of."

"Yes," said Jane, "but what else? Mike?"

"It takes honesty to look at myself and see who I really am," said Mike.

"Imagine honesty as Timmy's light that shines on all the important parts of our lives," said Jane. Her eyes became sad and her shoulders hunched over, as if remembering the demons of her past. "My past behavior, my mistakes, my sins and errors, the people I've hurt, my secrets and my fears. Until I learn to recognize my mistakes, I have no hope of fixing them."

She looked at me and dropped her guard for just a moment. I could see the pain in her face.

That evening, Leon was chairing an AA meeting in our apartment. When time for sharing came, my hand went up. Leon winked as he called on me. I had seen many of my chums breaking house rules, coming in late, pushing the envelope wherever possible.

"Look," I said, "some of you guys have been, well, bending the rules. Small things mostly, but I've decided that for me, they are the first step down a slippery slope. So, starting right now, I'm going to follow the rules. Quit pushing the limits. No more white lies or stretching the truth. In fact, no lies of any kind. If I'm going to get better, I have to get honest." I looked up at twelve men, all staring at me as if I'd lost my mind.

The next day, I tiptoed around, watching my language and behavior carefully, and that night I proudly announced to Leon that I had succeeded in my efforts at honesty for one day.

"One day at a time," said Leon with another wink.

However, in group the next day, I felt a lie form up in my mouth like a fish. Of its own accord, it jumped out of my mouth and flopped around on the floor. I was aghast. My counselor and the others in the group recognized the lie at once and booed me soundly. Yet, in my embarrassment, my old way of thinking kept me from admitting what I had just done. Finally, that afternoon I had to seek out my counselor because my conscience was killing me.

"Today in group, I, uh, misspoke." It was the kindest way to say I had lied. My counselor looked at me and smiled.

"I'm glad you're learning to tell the difference," she said.

Leon was waiting for me in the hallway.

"If you wink at me one more time, I'll hit you," I said, "and that's no lie."

Openness

"What's next?" I asked as we settled back in the apartment after a long day at the center.

"Openness," said Mike. "You must become open to new ideas." He sipped his coffee and looked like he wanted a cigarette. "Since everything you think you know about life is wrong, you must throw out all those broken ideas and replace them with ones that work."

"What do you mean, openness?" I asked.

"Keeping an open mind," said Reggie, putting his feet up on the couch. "Open to new ways of seeing the world."

"What's wrong with my old way?" I asked, realizing my mistake even as the words left my mouth.

"My friend," said Mike condescendingly, "if you'll recall, it was your old way of thinking that got you here in the first place. Your old thinking was insanity let loose upon the world."

"Yeah," I said. "I forgot about that part."

"In our old lives," said Reggie, "our opinions were pretty much fixed, since we knew we had all the right answers. Our arrogance wouldn't let others be more right than we were."

"Okay," I said; "How do I do this?"

"Won't be easy. We hold onto our opinions fiercely, even when they lead us into negative consequences," said my friend Mike. "Since new thinking will ruin your drinking, your mind will hold on to old ideas at any cost. You'll hear yourself saying something like' I never did that', or 'This can't be right', or 'Yes, but.'"

The morning dawned gray and overcast. I pulled the covers up and hugged myself. It felt good to wake up sober. Maybe this was going to work after all. I slid from my warm bed and put on the coffee. In a few minutes, we were on our way to breakfast.

"That reminds me," said Mike, "about last night."

"Criminy!" I said. "At least wait until we eat."

"The tide and your character defects wait for no man," he intoned.

"Go on," said Timmy. "I wanna hear."

"Well, just for Timmy," Mike smiled. "Okay, I repeat, open-mindedness."

"What about it?" I asked.

"You don't have it," said Mike. "As addicts and alcoholics, we're some close-minded SOBs. We'll argue a point until we're blue in the face. Our mind is made up long before anyone begins to speak. You wouldn't change your mind if it hare-lipped Granny and all her poor relations."

"Whoa!" I said. "Am I really that bad?"

"You are," said Robert, wiping the sleep from his eyes. "And worse."

"And me, too?" asked Timmy, wanting to be one of the boys.

"Yes, you, too," said Mike softly "It's a trait we all share."

Reggie came up alongside us as we entered the cafeteria.

"As a kid, I ached for the approval of others," Robert said. "If I knew everything, I thought people would like me, so I became an expert on whatever you were talking about. To maintain my sense of intellectual superiority, I had to defend my ideas against all comers."

"How long ago was this?" asked Mike. "I mean, since you were a kid?"

"About six weeks ago," said Robert, smiling.

"And what about my need to be right all the time?" asked Reggie.

"The trouble with that," said Mike, "is that if I'm right, then everybody else has to be wrong. And then…?"

"…then there's no reason for me to listen to the good advice of others," I admitted.

Jettison fixed ideas

The next morning when we met with Matt, Leon was exploring his new ideas.

"The words of Jesus provide a good example for completely reversing our ideas about life," said Leon, grinning. "Entirely new thinking replaces ideas that existed since the time of my buddy Moses. I know this may sound heretical for a son of Abraham, but it's true. For example, Jesus replaced an eye for an eye with love thy neighbor. And who can forget, He that is without sin among you, let him cast the first stone? He turned the world upside down and created a new way of thinking and living."

"We're spirits in search of ourselves," said Matt. "We live in the world, but are not of it. If we have a motto as recovering addicts and alcoholics, it should be this: Question everything."

"What do you mean?" asked Timmy. "When I was above the rules, I was in the back of the pharmacy shooting up Ritalin."

"There's a huge difference, my friend, between ignoring the rules of life and questioning the old concepts that got me into trouble," said Matt. "I need to be open to examining all the old ideas my brain has accumulated."

"Fixed ideas are the downfall of all sentient beings," added Robert, in one of his pontificating moods.

"Am I sentient?" asked Timmy.

"Sometimes I wonder," chortled Robert.

"I think what we're trying to say here is that we must be seekers," said Matt. "Seekers after truth wherever we find it. Without trying to define the nature of existence, we're simply looking for answers that make sense and are practical."

"'Beauty is Truth, Truth Beauty,'" said Reggie. "'That is all ye know on earth, and all ye need to know.' Keats, I think."

"Very good, preacher," said Matt. "I think Keats was right. When we question all things of importance, we're really seeking the beauty of existence."

"More than that," said Reggie, "we can't allow our ideas to become fixed, because when we think we have absolute knowledge, we've closed our minds to new ideas and new experiences."

"And to the flow of love from God," said Leon. "The sin that cannot be forgiven."

"Exactly," said Matt. "Cutting ourselves off from the light."

"So, with open hearts and minds," said Leon, "with beauty consciousness on our brows, we look to find a Higher Power that works in our lives every day.."

"Exactly," said Matt. "To ignore the questions of life is to opt out of life itself with all its beauty and joy. 'The unexamined life is not worth living.' I think that was Emerson."

"Ahem," chimed Robert and Mike as one.

"Uh, I think that may have been Socrates," said Robert.

"Thanks for refreshing my memory. Of course, it was Socrates," said Matt. "One last thought, then: Be a revolutionary."

Willingness

At breakfast, Mike asked, "But are you truly willing?"

"What do you mean, willing?" I asked.

"Would you stand on your head in the middle of Peachtree Street in downtown Atlanta, eating chocolate cake?" asked Mike.

"Huh?" one of my more spiritual replies in those days.

"Would you go to Montana and shine shoes for a year?" asked Robert. "Well, would you?"

"Wait a minute! What's chocolate cake and shining shoes got to do with recovery?" I asked.

"Exactly this," said Mike. "You have no idea what's good for you. If you listen to what your diseased mind is telling you, you'll use again."

"And if you use again, you'll die," said Robert.

"Okay," I said. "I'm willing to change. Admittedly I don't know how, but I assume someone will tell me, right?"

"Right," said Robert. "For example, you have to accept that you're not the doctor anymore. Now you're the patient. You have to admit to yourself that you're the sick one."

I grimaced but nodded. "That's an awful lot to swallow all at one time," I said.

"Not really," said Robert, "you just have to become willing to become willing. One little bit at a time."

"That sounds easier," I said. "But what if I can't...?"

"Failure is no longer an option," said Mike.

Robert returned to the cafeteria line and came back, smiling, with a large chocolate brownie.

"Hey, guys!" He was grinning from ear to ear. "Three frogs are sitting on a log. One decides to jump in the water. How many are left?"

I must have looked at Robert like a fool. Both he and Mike busted out laughing. Mike held up three fingers.

"Huh," I stammered.

"Three. One made a decision, but he never did anything about it."

"Like a lot of people in the program," nodded Robert, my jolly clown. "They make a decision to live a better life, but never do."

"It takes more than willingness," said Mike, again holding up three fingers. "Let's review," he said. "One: honesty above all else. Two: become open to new ideas. And three: became willing to change."

"I'm willing to accept that," I said, grinning. "Now I'm going potty. I'm willing to do that."

"If you're willing to try," shouted Mike as I walked away, "all doors will open for you."

Begin with Baby Steps

Ego deflation is a requirement for finding
our place in the world.

We must find new eyes to view the world
in a new way.

We discovered knowledge from unconventional
sources, distinct from head knowledge.

We found a measure of serenity when we quit
fighting the world and flowed with it.

Honesty is the first and most essential step in
overcoming our disease.

Openness to new ideas and new ways of
thinking followed.

We found we could jettison the old ways of
thinking that had nearly destroyed us.

Willingness to change enabled us
to move forward.

Practical Ideas

"The whole secret of existence
is to live without fear."
—*The Buddha*

Ask for help

It was Jane's turn again. I had taken to sitting in the front of the room, thinking I should keep my friends close and my enemies closer. The topic today was asking for help. Jane was staring straight at me over the top of her granny glasses.

"Well," she said, reminding me ever so much of my ex-mother-in-law, who worked part-time as a harpy. "Why couldn't you ask for help, Linville?" She stood accusingly in front of me, looking for any excuse to whack me.

"No macho doctor would ever admit to any personal shortcomings," I said. "Besides, I was afraid you'd discover that I was hooked on drugs."

"Uh, Ms. Jergens, I mean, er, Jane," said Timmy. "Doesn't asking for help necessarily imply a certain measure of humility?"

She turned to Timmy and smiled. "Yes, something Linville clearly lacks."

Robert leaned over and whispered in my ear, "Humility, I've been told, can be defined as a clear knowledge and acceptance of my place in the universe."

Shed resentments

Harold was still in his first few days of rehab when Mike cornered him in the apartment before breakfast. Harold had just moved into the empty bed in my room. He was growing visibly angrier each day.

"Give me your car keys," said Mike, his hand extended toward Harold.

"Why should I?" growled Harold.

"Because you're so angry, I'm afraid you might hurt yourself."

Harold fumed for a moment, then took a deep breath and sat down.

"You're right," he said, handing over his keys. "Last night all I could think about was parking on the railroad tracks and waiting for the train."

"Do you know why you're so angry?" I asked.

"Sure," said Harold. "All I can think about is my ex-partner back in Macon. He's the cause of all of my problems."

As he spoke, his face became livid. I thought I saw his back arch up.

"He's the one that turned me into the Medical Board. My whole life is ruined and he's the cause. The bastard stabbed me in the back."

Robert was sitting on the couch munching loudly on a bag of chips. He wiped his fingers on his pants and began to speak.

"You know," he said, "you don't have to be so angry. I know how to get rid of your resentment."

"Oh, yeah?" Harold blurted out, almost shouting. "How?"

"You do know what a resentment is, don't you?" Robert asked, throwing the empty chip bag at the trashcan and missing.

"No!" Harold countered, "but I'm sure you're about to tell me."

"Calm down there, doc," said Mike. "He's only trying to help."

Harold crossed his arms over his chest and shut up.

"A resentment is when I harbor ill feelings against someone for something I think they did to me," said Robert.

"…and hold on to those feelings," said Mike, "until they become a ball and chain tying me to that person and filling me with an anger so strong it overwhelms my thinking."

"Holding on to a resentment is like drinking poison and expecting the other person to die," said Robert.

Harold closed his eyes and shook his head. "So, what do I do?"

"There's a simple prayer that a friend taught me," Robert said.

Harold rolled his eyes, but said nothing.

"Every night before you go to bed, I want you to get down on your knees, fold your hands, and close your eyes. Thank God for all the good things that happened during your day. Then, say, God, I thank you for taking away the resentment I feel against my partner and replacing it with the faith that no matter what happens, everything will be all right. Got that?"

"The part about faith is important," said Mike, "because you don't want to leave an empty hole when the resentment disappears."

"The whole thing sounds pretty silly to me," said Harold.

"Do it once a day for fourteen days," Robert said, "and I guarantee your resentment will be gone."

Some days later Harold reported back on his progress.

"You seem a lot calmer these days," I said. Harold nodded.

"I think Robert's prayer must have worked," he said. "I don't exactly feel love toward my ex-partner, but my anger is no longer consuming me."

Mike reached into his pocket, pulled out Harold's car keys, and threw them across the table to his roommate.

Don't isolate

Jane's session. "The unavoidable consequence of my using was isolation," she said, waxing philosophical. "I was terrified that someone might discover my drinking. No one could possibly understand the problems I faced nor how overwhelming was my need to find relief. In time, I withdrew from all my friends and coworkers."

I recalled the last year of my using. I never asked anyone over unless they used. In time I only invited people who injected cocaine. At the end, I wandered the house, needle in my arm, seeing no one. I stopped answering the phone. I just wanted to be alone with my drugs. My gods were Lady Cocaine and John Barleycorn and they permitted no other gods before them.

"The worst consequence of my growing isolation was that all, and I do mean all, of my relationships became broken," said Jane. "Family, friends, social connections, everybody. One of the most important parts of your healing will be restoring these neglected relationships."

"Dr. Taylor says recovery is the process of re-people-izing," said Timmy. "I guess that's what he means."

Become dependable

I met with Cameron in her office. Today we were to face the monster of my ex-wife and ask to see my young daughters. On her wall was a diploma which read, Master's Degree, Psychological Counseling.

"How often have you seen your girls in the last year?" asked Cameron.

"Once or twice," I answered, embarrassed.

"Why?"

"I don't know." I felt anger rising within me. "Yeah, I do know—my using was more important than my children."

"Good to know that," said Cameron. "What makes you think your ex-wife will let you see them now?"

I exploded. "What do you mean? I have a separation agreement that says ..."

"Whoa, stop!" cried Cameron. "Have you forgotten where you are? You're a patient in a mental hospital, for crying out loud! You may have changed lately, but to your family, you're still an undependable drunk."

I bit my lip and let my counselor take over. In a few moments, she had my ex-wife on the phone.

"What would it take," she asked her, "to begin trusting the children's father again?" The answer was much simpler than I could possibly have imagined.

"If he would just show up when he says he will," said the mother of my children. "If he says he'll be here at five o'clock on Friday, then he shows up at five o'clock on Friday." I was flabbergasted.

Find a sponsor

Standing in front of his desk, Matt seemed out of sorts today, grumpy even.

"Enough bitching and moaning!" his voice close to shouting. "If you think you can do this thing all by yourself, well, why don't you." He took a deep breath to calm himself, but his eyes were still pointed and sharp.

"In other words," he said, "you need a sponsor who can help you work the Steps, because you can't do this thing by yourself. You must find someone who has been down this road before and can show you how it's done."

He turned and walked around his desk, sat down, and took a large pull off his coffee before he spoke again.

"Interestingly, sponsorship is not mentioned anywhere in the Big Book, but over the past seventy years, it's become an essential part of the program. The role of a sponsor is clear: they help you work the Steps. They don't give you a ride to meetings, lend you money, or buy you dinner, although they may do all these things and more. In time, they can become a confidant, a guide, a mentor, and a friend. They will give freely of their time and energy. But their job is this and this only—to help you work the Steps."

Timmy raised his hand.

"Yes, Timmy," said Matt.

"How do I find a sponsor?" he asked.

"It's easy," Matt said. "When you get home, at the end of your first meeting, raise your hand, introduce yourself to the group, and say you need a temporary sponsor. Someone always responds. They may or may not be your permanent sponsor, but they will be your lifeline to sobriety until something better comes along."

He paused and looked sadly out the window. When he resumed, his voice was softer and kinder.

"Later, you'll hear someone who has what you want. That's the person you want for your sponsor. Ask them."

Matt smiled. To be sure, it wasn't much of a smile, but it was a smile.

"Constant contact with your sponsor is a necessity. You must speak with them in person or on the phone every day. You must be absolutely and completely honest with them. You must be willing to share your deepest feelings and your most horrible memories. You must trust and respect them; they will lead you on a pathway you cannot see and don't understand. They got here the same way you did, they'll understand who you are, what you did, and what you need to do to get sober."

"I'm sorry, folks," he said, looking as if he was going to cry. "I just found out that one of my first sponsees killed himself. He was a paratrooper, Special Forces, with disabling PTSD."

Go to meetings

We were at a meeting in Buckhead, the major party zone in Atlanta. A man named Kenny was telling his story. He looked a thousand years old, but his eyes still twinkled. He reminded me of my grandfather.

"I discovered that I had to be hands-on in my recovery," he said. "I couldn't just hang back and expect sobriety to come to me. I had to chase after it with all my heart. Slipping into a meeting after the Serenity Prayer, sitting quietly in the back of the room, speaking to nobody, then slipping out just as quietly before the Lord's Prayer—that ain't gonna cut it!"

"My sponsor said I should hang out with the ones who have their shit together and listen to what they have to say. Avoid the losers. It won't take long to tell the difference. As a newcomer, go to a meeting every day. Arrive early and meet people. Stay late and help clean up. This is your new home, said my sponsor, love it and take care of it."

"Find a home group where people can get to know you. You can share your problems with them, and you'll learn to listen. In these rooms, I don't have to wear a mask. I can be who I am. Fellowship is a wonderful part of the AA life."

Work the Steps

Timmy and I were visiting Father Mick. We were talking about the Steps of AA.

"Why do we work the Steps?" said Father Mick. "Let me count the ways." He began to list them.

"I worked the Steps because…They took away the pain…They gave me hope…They gave me the psychic change I needed…They helped me find forgiveness…They helped me deal with my past…They helped me overcome my fear and my character defects…They helped me find a higher power I could relate to…They helped me understand my disease…They provided treatment for a disease that was killing me…They returned me to my family and gave me new friends…They taught me how to pray and meditate…They gave me back my self-respect…They helped me understand the insanity of my disease."

He stopped and looked us in the eye. "I worked the Steps because they saved my life."

Spiritual awakening

Dr. Taylor was addressing the assembled drunks and junkies. Today another crop of impaired physicians was about to reenter the world. This was Taylor's last chance to impart some small measure of recovery wisdom.

"We were morally bankrupt," he said. "Our lives had become filled with lies, deceit, and controlling behavior. We neglected our responsibilities, ignored the consequences of our actions, and gave up what morals we had left to serve the gods of our addiction."

"Our drinking and drugging produced a psychic change all right, but it was a fatal one. After a few hits, we were amazed at how good we felt. We didn't regret the past nor wish to shut the door on it. We comprehended the word serenity and knew peace. Our whole attitude and outlook upon life changed. It was our solution for living. But it was killing us."

"We were afflicted by a soul sickness. If we could but heal that sickness of the heart, the mind and body would follow. But without such a deep-seated change, abstinence was utterly useless. We had to dethrone our ego with its false ideas about life and develop a whole new manner of living. A complete change in character was required. This is nothing less than the death of the old person and the rebirth of a healthy soul. This psychic change must be complete and overwhelming. Here, we are talking about a total change in the direction in our thinking and our behavior."

"This spiritual awakening is not an event, rather it is a process, a life-long journey. Each day will bring a fuller understanding of our place in the universe and a deeper relationship with our Higher Power. Our long-neglected spirituality, one definition of our relationship with God, will slowly become functional. We will practice these principles in all our affairs. Don't worry, it's not as hard as it sounds. And it will save your life."

Practical Ideas

Unable to overcome our using by ourselves, we learned to ask for help.

We discovered the value of a sponsor's help.

Going to self-help meetings, such as AA and NA, provided needed support.

We learned the danger of holding resentments and how to shed them.

Isolation made things worse.

We learned how to become dependable.

The Steps gave us the tools we needed to change our thinking and behavior and find a life of peace and joy.

We began the process of psychic rearrangement.

This is what is meant by a spiritual awakening.

Moral Inventory

"This is the very perfection of a man,
To find out his own imperfections."
—*Augustine*

Earlier, Father Mick had told us that an essential step in changing our character was to admit to our mistakes and be willing to share that confession with another person—and with God.

"Now," said Father Mick, "you've reached a point where you have to inventory your past. By doing this, you'll discover what your character defects are, and you'll know what you need to work on."

"Oh, shit," said Timmy.

"Easy, Tim," said Father Mick. "It's not as tough as it sounds. Remember, baby steps."

"Right," said Timmy. "Baby steps."

The good priest continued, "Leave no bit of backwater undisturbed.

Turn over every old rotten log and poke into every crevice. Write everything out longhand. Don't dictate or keyboard. There's something important about writing it out with pen and paper, some connection is made that's essential. Don't argue your side or try to make yourself look good. We're not about defending ourselves or pleading our case. We're after the plain, unadorned facts."

"I'm afraid," said Timmy.

"Of what?" asked Father Mick.

"Afraid of sharing my secrets," Timmy said. "I always thought I'd take them with me to my grave."

"If you do that," Father Mick said, "you'll go to your grave drunk. The only real secret in AA is that everybody has the same secret. Besides, when you tell on your disease, it loses power over you."

Mike and I had driven across Atlanta to a small meeting in the courtyard of a church near the University campus. It was called the Starlight meeting because, weather permitting, it was held under the stars. Mike was standing just outside the door with a newcomer named Mark. Mark was 20-ish, styled in hip-hop clothes and dreads. He looked uncomfortable, unable to go into the room.

"The things I've done are…are unforgivable," said Mark. His eyes were so full of pain I thought he might cry. "There's no hope for me," he said. "No way I can ever find forgiveness."

"Nah," said Mike. "Look in there," he said, pointing into the meeting room. At least fifty people milling around, waiting for the meeting to start. "Every person in there brought a secret with him that was too horrible to bear and too awful to share. Everyone. Look at them now."

We gazed at the crowd. They were laughing, joking, obviously not burdened by overwhelming guilt.

"The only real secret in this room is that everybody has a secret," said Mike. "What Joe did was no worse than what Charlie thought about. What Annie thought was no worse than what Mary did. We're all basically the same. We have the same wants, the same fears, and the same hopes and dreams. This is the only place in the world where you don't have to wear a mask. Come in and join us. You have nothing to lose but your misery."

Mark still looked uncertain.

"C'mon," said Mike, "the coffee's free. If you don't feel better, we'll give you twice your misery back." Mark laughed uncertainly. We went in together

Sitting at our dinner table that night, Timmy began writing his moral inventory. Two hours later, his fingers were sore, but he had filled seven pages with descriptions of his resentments and wrongdoings.

"I want to throw up," he said. "This really hurts."

"Maybe it's time to quit for the night," I said. "Here, give me your pad." I put it up on a shelf.

Timmy came back the next night and worked for another two hours.

"How much more do I have to do?" he asked. "How many pages did you end up with?"

"Most of the guys end up with about twenty pages," I said. "But the number of pages isn't important. Much better you should get all the big chunks out."

The next night, Timmy finished up with twenty-two pages. He threw the yellow pad down in disgust. "I know I did all that stuff," he said, "but I sure don't like seeing it on paper."

"Good job," I said. "This step generally separates the winners from the losers. Failing to complete the inventory has sent many an alcoholic back to the bar. Congratulations. Now you're ready to read it to somebody."

"Ugh," said Timmy.

The next morning, Timmy made an appointment with his counselor to read what he had written.

I waited eagerly for Timmy to return from his confession. When he did, he looked relieved. He threw the pages he had written into the trash and flopped down on the couch.

"I'm tired," he said. "I hope I never have to do that again. hy do I have to read all my junk to another person? Why can't I just tell God and be done with it?"

"The answer to that is simple," I said. "It doesn't work."

"Oh," said Timmy.

"Okay, Tim," I said, "now go meditate on your list of wrongdoings, on why you did each thing, and how it felt to dump your garbage. Meditate for at least an hour then come back and you can start working on your character defects."

Character defects

Timmy dutifully returned from his meditation just before dinner. We were having spaghetti with meatballs, a favorite among the guys in our apartment. As I stirred the sauce, Timmy sat down at the table, yellow pad and pencil in hand.

"I'm hungry," he said. "Let's get started so we can eat."

"For each of your misdeeds, now confessed," said Robert, "select the character faults that were the basis for each one. You want to end up with a list of defects, so we'll know what to tackle next."

"In other words, generate a list of my character defects based on the mistakes I made."

"Right. I began by making a list of all the character defects I could think of."

"Like picking out ice cream at Baskin-Robbins. I got it," said Timmy.

"I started with the seven deadly sins and added some more."

"The seven deadly sins...?"

"Wrath, greed, sloth, pride, lust, envy, and gluttony. But you might want to add resentment, cowardice, self-pity, dishonesty, jealousy, envy, intolerance, stuff like that."

I served the spaghetti while Timmy wrote. He finished in just over an hour and handed me his tomato-stained sheets.

"Any surprises?" asked Robert.

"I've known about most of my character defects for a long time," he said. "But I found myself writing down 'selfishness' over and over. I never thought of myself as being selfish, but it's hard to deny when it's right there in black and white. Timmy's a selfish person," he said, "but I can work on that, right?"

Moral bankruptcy

"We were morally bankrupt," said Cameron, leading the morning spiritual. "We, all of us, severed our relationship with anything that would interfere with our using. Whatever had passed for a Higher Power in our lives before our addiction took hold, was now long gone. We turned away from any and every source of spiritual guidance. With no moral compass, we were lost and alone in our despair."

She took a deep breath and looked out at our smiling faces.

"Viewed as a spiritual problem," she continued, "addiction is the false sense of separation from God."

Some days I was more confused than others. Today was a case in point.

"Okay," said Matt standing in front of the group. "Answer this question for me. What is moral bankruptcy?"

For some reason, I felt it necessary to express my ignorance in public. "I understand that in the worldly sense, bankruptcy means financial ruin," I said, "but I don't see …"

Wee Willy spoke up. "You're daft, man. Have ye never woken on a cold damp floor with no idea how you got there?"

"Or found yourself in bed with a strange naked woman," said someone in the back, "and can't find your car keys—hell, can't find your car?"

"I know my life's a disaster," I said.

"Good," said Matt, "keep going."

"I always thought of myself as a moral man," I said, "but I …"

Wee Willy was getting angry. "What a load of shite! Even I know my moral compass is out of whack. It's just that on most days I really don't give a tinker's damn."

"If my moral compass is 180 degrees out of kilter," said Matt, circling his desk, "then it will take a huge psychological displacement to correct the path I've been on."

"Yes, but …" I said.

"Shut up," said my friend Mike sitting beside me, "and listen."

"I knew you could get addicted to cocaine," said William, a cardiac surgeon with visions of grandeur. "But I knew I could handle it. After all, I'm a physician, right? But bad things, left to themselves, always get worse, they say. I made up excuses for the withdrawals from the office checking account that I used to pay my dealer. I stole syringes from the office to shoot up. I took narcotics from the office supply and lied about it to my head nurse. I had an affair with one of my nurses. I told my wife I was working late at the hospital. With just a little practice, lying came easy."

Matt turned to me. "Starting to understand?"

William's words were like a sword stuck deep in my heart. I opened my mouth to speak but nothing came out.

Matt questioned Wee Willy. "Tell us about your practice. You're a podiatrist, right?"

"Daggers, man," he said, "you're right on. I can cut toenails with the best of 'em. And I'm particularly good at the surgery. I can find a hundred reasons to operate. Sure, the government busybodies are always on my butt, but so what? I kept enough private rich ladies to keep me in whiskey. My favorite patients brought me a fifth of single malt every time they came to the office. A little sweet talk and a few kisses on the cheek, you know. For the very best and wealthiest patients, I made house calls. A little of the old in-and-out never hurt a lonely widow."

"So, it seems. Tell us what brought you here," said Matt.

"You don't want to hear that tired old story, do ya?" he replied.

"I think we do," said Matt.

"Okay then," said Wee Willy. "The auditor caught me educating one of my female patients in the gentle art of fellatio. The auditor said I had whiskey on my breath, but I swear she was drunker than I was."

"Well," said Matt, looking at me. "Are you getting the picture?"

I squirmed, knowing I had done many of the things Wee Willy described.

"Yes," I said, unable to look Matt in the face.

We turned away from the light

Stephen was a born-again preacher whose best friend was Jack Daniels. His language was full of Biblical references, which bothered me, but he was fun to listen to.

"You lost the light," he told me. We were sitting on the porch outside the apartment.

"I'm not sure he ever had it, Stephen," said Robert.

"What do you mean?" I asked.

"You turned away from God, from his light," Stephen said, "and took up living in the darkness."

The darkness part made sense.

"When we turn away from God, we lose his help. We're lost and alone," said Stephen. "Without the light of his word, we grow cold and weary."

He had the cold and weary part right, too.

"Tell me about this light," I said.

"The light is the love of God," Stephen said. "Without that love, we live in fear."

"Why didn't your God reach out and help me?" I asked. "I certainly could have used it."

"He doesn't butt in," said Stephen. "He's a polite gentleman, the kindly uncle who won't interfere unless you ask for help."

"I thought ..."

"If you want to have a conversation with God," he said, "you'll have to turn around and face the light."

I needed help, but I wasn't sure about facing the light. I had been dodging the truth for a long time.

Suddenly, I remembered a conversation I had with Sarah, a counselor I met in detox. She struggled to find her sobriety, she told me. The last time she got drunk, she sat at the end of the bar and drank until she closed the place down. She took a taxi home, and, in her drunkenness, she prayed, 'God, does this mean we can't have a relationship?' To her surprise, she heard an answer as clear as day. "No, but it makes it more difficult."

Could it be true that my using did block the light?

Fear

We were walking back to the apartments after an AA meeting at the detox wing. The topic had been fear.

"Fear cancels out all the good things in life," said Mike. "I can marry the most beautiful woman in the world, but if I'm afraid of losing her, my life will suck. I can be elected chairman of the board, but if I'm afraid of the vice-chairman's ambition for my job, I won't have serenity. Fear brings out the worst in me. Every fault of character I possess will blossom on a diet of fear. The fruit of fear is anxiety, stress, indigestion, and headache."

"Where does fear come from?" I asked.

"Deep in your subconscious," said Vera, walking alongside me.

"The natural state of man?" asked Robert.

"I don't think so," said Vera. "I think the natural state of man is to be happy, joyous, and free of fear."

"Hmm," said Timmy, "My mother used to say that a little fear was good for you, but she quit driving because she was afraid of turning left across the traffic. I love you, Mom, but ..."

"Father Mick said that faith replaces fear," quoted Robert.

"So, where do I get this faith thing?" I asked, trying to be flippant. "Do they sell it like a relic at the corner cathedral? Is it hidden in the bottom of a Cracker Jack box?"

"O, ye of little faith," quipped Robert. "Laugh not, lest ye be laughed at."

Vera waved and headed off toward the women's apartments.

"My little brother," said Mike, "you're a long way from understanding the meaning of faith. Just know that you need it badly, and if you come back in about fifty pages, you'll find it. As for today, don't drink, go to meetings, and have fun."

"Yes, master," I said.

"Matt said that fear isn't rational," said Timmy from the back of the group. "What'd he mean?"

"Timmy, me boy," said Wee Willy, "none of our emotions are rational. They all spring from the heart, where rationality is given short shrift."

"What're you talking about?" asked Timmy, starting to get irritated.

"Easy, Timmy," I said. "Wee Willy's right. The mind is the rational part of us. It does calculations, measurements, and projections, but the mind can't feel. The heart, on the other hand, is the source of our creativity, our inspiration. It houses our emotions, which are never rational."

"The point is, Timmy fella," said Wee Willy, "your emotions are yers an' yers alone. They must be accepted for wat they are. Your mind can argue facts, but no one can argue wi' your emotions."

"That's the problem with fear," I said. "I can't think my way out of it."

"No, you can't," Robert said.

We walked along in silence. When we reached the breezeway at the apartments, Stephen was there and we continued our conversation.

"Fear exists only in my head," said Stephen, when we brought him up to date on our conversation. "I was surprised when I learned that the opposite of love is not hate, but fear."

"False Expectations Appearing Real," said Timmy, repeating Matt's words.

"All my fears can be reduced to three," said Stephen. "Fear of not getting what I want. Fear of losing what I have. And fear that if you knew who I really was, you wouldn't like me."

We went inside and I put on a pot of coffee.

"Fear drives my thinking into negativity of all kinds," Stephen continued. "It triggers all my character defects—lust, gluttony, greed, anger—you name it. Fear pushes me to chase material success, financial security, and recognition. It makes me want to control the world. I try to overcome my fear by exaggerating my own importance. My low self-esteem fuels my fear of never being good enough."

Timmy, sitting on the couch, looked puzzled. "But…how…do…I?"

"With prayer, Timmy," said Leon, stirring sugar into his coffee. "My rebbe taught it to me. 'God, I thank you for taking away my fear, and replacing it with the faith that no matter what happens, everything will be alright.' The key is to recognize when I'm afraid and then remember to say the prayer."

"I think your rebbe was right!" said Stephen.

At morning check-in, Timmy told us about his dream. It was scary.

"I was a child again, sleeping alone in my mother's bed. Everything was dark and I was afraid. I was sure something terrible was about to happen. Something evil was in the room with me. Frightened half to death, I peeked quickly under the bed and a witch, black as night and with eyes like burning red coals, came screaming out from under the bed and flew around the room then came straight at me. I pulled the covers over my head, but I was helpless. I screamed so loud that I woke myself up. I was in a cold sweat and my heart was racing a hundred miles an hour. But none of it was real," he said. "It was all in my head."

We were in Cameron's class again. The room was packed, for she was wearing a red dress that looked painted on and her neckline was dangerously low.

"I always thought that hatred was the opposite of love," she said. "But I was to learn that hate was just another negative emotion, alongside envy, jealousy, and the rest. I was told that to have the life I wanted, I had to remove all the negative thoughts from my mind. To be happy, they said, I could no longer afford to hate anything, not any person, place, or thing."

All the males in the room clapped.

At lunch, Reggie shared his experience with prayer. "I can remember when I learned that prayer could remove my fear," said Reggie, holding forth in his best preacher voice. "It happened one day while I was sitting in a courtroom waiting for my case to come up. Of course, I was innocent, but that didn't stop me from being afraid."

All of us around the lunch table laughed.

"I arrived in the courtroom at 7:30 in the morning," he said, "and took a seat on a wooden bench. I had never been in court before as a defendant and I was frightened. My case didn't come up until almost 1 pm, so I was there for hours. Every little sound or noise would set off a crazy fear that leaped into my belly and sent shock waves through the rest of my body.

So, I prayed, 'God, I thank you for taking away my fear and replacing it with the faith that no matter what happens, everything will be all right.' Immediately, the fear would melt away and I could breathe again. But within moments, the judge would look at me funny, or the bailiff would shuffle his feet, or someone would cough, and the fear would come screaming back.

So again, I'd say my little prayer and again the fear would leave. This happened over and over again, maybe fifty times. The young man sitting next to me looked at me like I was crazy, then got up and moved away, but I kept praying."

"The power of prayer," I said. "Working in the real world."

"And it worked every time?" asked Timmy.

"Yep," said Reggie. "Every time."

Summer was hot and the air conditioning in the cafeteria felt good. Mike and I were having lunch.

"Why does life seem so hard?" I asked. About that time, the beautiful Cameron sat down beside us, only a salad on her tray.

"A good question," she said. "There are a lot of reasons why life might seem difficult," she said. "Can you think of any?" For a second I thought I was back in her newcomer's class.

"If I believe life is hard, my choices are pretty limited," said Mike. "One is to hide under the covers, avoiding as much pain as possible."

"Another would be to suppress everything about this life in anticipation of the next," I said.

"Or I could surround myself with all the worldly goods and power I can acquire, buffering myself from the pain of the world," said Cameron.

"Tried that," said Mike. "Didn't work."

"But what if I believe life is easy but still come home with a headache and a bruised ego?" asked Cameron. "What then?"

We sat silently, Mike and I, forks held in eager anticipation.

"I can think of two biggies that keep me from finding harmony," she said. "First, I'm not at peace with my place in the universe, and second, I'm afraid."

"My place in the universe, that's humility, right?" I ventured.

"All alone in a big scary world," mumbled Mike.

Go for the roots

"I had another weird dream last night," said Timmy, sitting at the kitchen table in the apartment. "I can't get it out of my head."

"Tell," I said, refilling my coffee.

"I was a lumberjack standing in front of a huge evergreen tree in the forest. My job was to trim the tree, removing all of its character defects. I shook the tree as hard as I could, dislodging most of the dead needles and debris."

"Is this good?" I asked.

"Yes," came the answer, "but not good enough."

"I then took a huge pruning saw and cut out all the dead wood I could find."

"Is this good?" I asked.

"Yes," came the answer, "but not good enough."

"Next I began to trim back all the small limbs, quite a bit."

"Is this good," I asked.

"Yes," came the answer, "but not good enough."

"At this point over half the tree had been trimmed but I persisted until only the major branches remained and they contained no green needles at all. I discarded the saw and took up an ax. Slashing and attacking, I removed the last of the main branches until only the trunk remained."

"Is this good?" I asked.

"Yes," came the answer, "but not good enough."

"Using all my strength, I felled the trunk until only the stump remained, relieved of most of its bark."

"Is this good?" I asked.

"Yes," came the answer, "but not good enough."

"The final attack was slower and more careful but just as fierce. I hewed and hammered and splintered until nothing of the giant tree remained above ground with only its roots below. I started to ask again but realized that I already knew the answer. I had done nothing to remove the roots that fed the tree."

"And what is the root that feeds this tree of your character defects," I asked, awaiting the answer we both knew.

"Fear," said Timmy. "Fear is the root that supports and nourishes the tree of my character defects. I must attack the root. I must find a way to live without fear."

Humility

Robert, John, and I were at the shopping center to get our monthly haircut. John was getting his usual crew cut. Robert and I sat flipping through old magazines as we waited.

Something was bothering me and I mentioned it to Robert.

"Huh?" said Robert. "You don't know what it means to become as a child?"

"No, honestly, I have no idea," I said. "I know it's said that to walk the spiritual path, I need to become as a child. I've repeatedly asked the question but have never gotten a satisfactory answer. Is it because children have big heads and they look cute? Is it because they're innocent? Innocence never got very far in my book. Besides, aren't they little King Babies? What gives?"

"It's quite simple, actually," said John. "The thing that marks a child most characteristically, and that the child knows with painful clarity, is that it needs help. For almost everything in life, the child is dependent on others and must ask for help. In the adult world, we have forgotten just how powerless we really are and how dependent we are on others. A child knows what we are afraid to admit, that it has to ask for help."

A good definition for humility, I thought.

The afternoon Georgia sky had turned black and dumped thunder and rain, but the overhead lights and the smile on Cameron's face lit up the room.

"If I think I have humility, I have it not," said Cameron. She smiled at Mike and me. "Like serenity, it comes unbidden when the heart is ready and not before. I can't pursue it. Like all spiritual ideas, the word escapes rational definition. It's often described as the virtuous opposite of pride. It's tied up with the concepts of selflessness, calmness, and serenity in the face of adversity. The best way I can describe the idea is through the words of those far wiser than I."

She read from a handout:

"Humility is perfect quietness of heart. It is to expect nothing, to wonder at nothing that is done to me, to feel nothing done against me. It is to be at rest when nobody praises me, and when I am blamed or despised. It is to have a blessed home in the Lord, where I can go in and shut the door, and kneel to my Father in secret and am at peace as in a deep sea of calmness, when all around and above is trouble."
—Andrew Murray

"There is no limit to the amount of good a man can do, as long as he does not care who takes the credit."
—Sunday-Bolorunduro Awoniyi

"We are here to add what we can to, not get what we can from, life."
—Sir William Osler

"Take my yoke upon you, and learn of me; for I am meek and lowly in heart: and ye shall find rest unto your souls."
—Matthew 11:29

Vera added, "Humility is being at peace with my place in the universe." Cameron nodded, looking at the storm outside.

"I want each of you to name one spiritual act that you can perform," she said.

"Cooking for the people you love," said Vera, her hair still damp from the rain.

"The fellowship of human connection," said one.

"Hands in the earth, gardening," said another.

"Connecting with nature, walking in the woods."

"Yoga."

"Puppies and unconditional love," I said.

Cameron asked us to name pathways that could lead a person to God.

Vera spoke first, drying her hair with her gym towel.

"Religion," she said. "Religion should take me to God."

"But how many of us have been abandoned by the religion of our fathers?" Cameron asked.

"Prayer," said a voice. "Prayer should lead us to God."

"But it's said, faith without works is dead, right?"

A murmur went through the group.

"Developing a set of moral principles would be a good start, I should think," said Vera.

"And which of these principles actually works in the real 9-to-5 world?" asked Cameron.

"We could become vegan and do yoga all day."

"And who's going to pay for all this spirituality?" asked Cameron. "How will you support yourself and your family while you're chasing nirvana?"

I started to speak when the shy, quiet woman in the corner, who had not said a word in any of our sessions with Cameron, spoke up.

"There are as many paths to heaven as there are people in his universe," she said.

"I like that," said Cameron. "Would you repeat it for those who were meditating or doing yoga in the back of the room?"

"There are as many pathways to God as there are people walking," she said, more forcefully, gaining the strength of her conviction. "No one is excluded."

Moral Inventory

As our using deepened, we found ourselves in a state of moral bankruptcy. We had abandoned all the virtues we admired.

We turned away from the light and lived in darkness.

We were consumed by fear which fueled all our harmful character defects.

Our newfound honesty allowed us to look deeply at the mistakes and misdeeds that filled our past.

We began to see how our character defects had resulted in our hurtful behavior.

Surprisingly, we discovered that prayer could remove our fears.

As we began to appreciate our place in the world, we experienced our first taste of humility.

Prayer and Meditation

"For what is prayer
but the expansion of yourself
into the living ether?"
—Kahlil Gibran

Meditation and prayer

"Sought through prayer and meditation to improve our conscious contact with God as we understood Him," said Father Mick. "Prayer and meditation. The Eleventh Step of AA." He was our guest at the Wednesday night AA meeting in our apartment. Timmy had cooked chili and Reggie made coleslaw and cornbread.

"I've heard people say that prayer is talking to God and meditation is listening," said Timmy.

"I've heard that, too," said Father Mick. "But I think they're parts of the same whole. Meditation clears and focuses my mind and sets the stage for prayer. Prayer addresses the issues I face today and asks for help in dealing with them. Together, they channel my thoughts and my actions into their most useful forms."

Timmy collected the plates and I poured coffee for the six men gathered around the goodly priest.

"So what is meditation?" asked Timmy, putting the dishes into the sink. "Yoga swamis at the airport chanting Hare Krishna?"

"No," laughed Father Mick. "Nothing like that. It's a simple technique to clear and focus the mind."

"Just meditate?" asked Timmy from the kitchen.

"Not just meditate," said Father Mick. "We meditate *on* something. Well, not just something. We meditate on God. About His nature, how I relate to Him, how I can live in His world."

"How do you do it?" asked Reggie, listening eagerly.

"I like to begin my day with a very simple prayer the moment I open my eyes. Something like, God, I thank you for waking me up, giving me life, and this wonderful world to live it in. I follow that with God, I thank you for keeping me clean and sober today. Then, after I'm dressed and have had at least two cups of coffee, I find a quiet comfortable place to sit."

"Do I have to sit cross-legged, you know, the lotus thing?" asked Timmy, getting down on the floor.

"You can," said Father Mick, "but sitting in a chair works fine, too. Whatever's comfortable, with your back straight. Get rid of everything which distracts you."

"Turn of the TV," said Timmy, nodding.

"Sit calmly for a few moments, close your eyes, and let the thoughts in your head die down," said Father Mick. "Don't be distracted by your mistakes from yesterday, your plans for the day, or your hopes for tomorrow."

He held up his coffee cup and I refilled it. I made the coffee extra strong just for him.

"Listen to the silence around you. Then turn your gaze inside. There is a calmness, maybe even a warmth there. Don't force it, let it come to you. When your mind and your body are quiet, open your eyes and pick up some spiritual reading material: The Bible, the Big Book, Touchstones for Men, maybe something by Rumi or Kahlil Gibran. Bill W. talks about using St. Francis' Prayer. Read each word slowly, savor each bite. Think about how can you apply what you've read to your daily life. and try to understand its deeper meaning."

"No speed reading," said Reggie, nodding.

"Think about each idea, mull it over slowly," said Father Mick.

"Meditate on it!" said Timmy.

"Just so," smiled Father Mick. "At this point, your body should be relaxed, your mind should be clear, and your attention focused on matters spiritual. Now you're ready to pray."

I sat silently, cross-legged on the floor, meditating on what I had heard.

Scientific prayer

"I still don't understand what faith is," I said, stirring my coffee. "Certainly not pink cherubs riding chariots drawn by winged horses, I hope."

"I agree," said Father Mick.

"My rebbe said that one definition of faith is success in prayer," said Leon. "I was having a terrible problem with anger and I went to see the rebbe. He gave me a prayer to say whenever my anger came bubbling up. I was skeptical at first, but I took his advice. I said the prayer and it worked. I was so excited I couldn't wait to try it again. Every time I said the prayer it worked! Now, I have faith that this prayer will be answered."

"Is any one form of prayer better than any other?" I asked, and immediately felt stupid.

"I suspect God loves to hear from all of us, whether by telegraph, telephone, or smoke signal. But yes," he said, "some have described what they call scientific prayer."

"Father Mick!" said Robert. "That sounds like an oxymoron. I thought science and spirituality were opposite ways of looking at the world."

"Those who know more about prayer than I, say that some prayers are more successful than others," he said. "They've sought out which forms are the most effective and discarded those that don't work as well."

"So prayer's, like a skill, or something?" asked Timmy.

Father Mick nodded. "The more you try your hand at prayer, the better your results will be. And the better your results, the more faith you'll have in the whole process."

"Like doing reps in the gym?" Robert ventured. I think he read about that in a fitness magazine.

"The psalmist says that prayers should always be in the form of thanksgiving," said Father Mick. "Since God knows what we need before we ask, we're actually thanking him for what he is already doing for us."

"Mike said I should say something like, 'God, I thank you for helping me do this or become that. Does that sound right?"

He nodded, tamped the tobacco down in his pipe, and lit it.

"The mystics also say that effective prayer requires a heart that's at peace. Don't come before the altar filled with resentments or ill feelings. But the single most important aspect is this—the more I believe that my prayer will work, the better it will work."

"So, prayer comes from the heart," said Timmy thoughtfully.

"Whatsoever ye shall ask in prayer, believing, ye shall receive," quoted Robert. "Matthew, I think."

The room fell quiet. After a few moments, the priest spoke.

"Another thing, prayer's like daily bread," said the priest. "It's only good for one day. Like eating and breathing, you must do it every day. It's one part of my daily dose of spirituality."

"It works," said Leon.

"What?" I asked.

"Prayer works," Leon repeated. "It changes things. Truly."

"It's the only thing I know of that can change a person's character," said Father Mick. "It's more concerned with changing me, than changing the world I live in."

"As I clean up my side of the street, my prayers should improve," Leon said.

"Of course," said Father Mick. "As I improve my inside, everything outside will improve as well. But the most important benefit of prayer is that it opens a relationship with God."

Father Mick stood up and held out his hands. "Would you care to join me?" he asked.

This group of ego-maniac men stood, held hands, and bowed their heads.

"God," said Father Mick, "I thank you for helping us to be the best persons today that we've ever been.

Becoming centered

Matt was trying to teach Timmy the art of becoming centered. It was Monday and I already wished it was Friday. A low energy day.

"Timmy," he asked, "how do you usually begin your day?"

"I would jump out of bed, shower as fast as I could, then grab a cup of coffee as I was going out the door. If I didn't pick up a honey bun on the way to work, I'd have one of my clerks fetch me a glazed donut. I could usually make it from my bed to my desk in less than forty-five minutes. Sometimes faster."

"What did you do when your day started going south?" Matt asked.

"You mean when my plans for the day got shot all to hell? I guess most days I got really irritable, slammed the phone down, that kinda stuff."

"How often did that happen?"

"Pretty much every day. I'd bitch at everyone around me, then go home and yell at the wife."

"And how did this work for you?"

"Not very well."

Matt turned to Mike.

"Mike," he asked, "Do you meditate in the mornings?"

"I try to, every morning," said Mike.

"When you meditate, what happens?"

"It clears my head and helps me focus. I end up in a place that's calm and comforting, where the cares of the world don't shout at me quite so loud. I lean back and bask in the glow. Later in the day, if I get upset or frazzled, I can reach back and pull that serenity into the present moment to calm myself."

"What happens if you forget your meditation?"

"By eleven o'clock, my day is pretty rough-edged."

"I think what Mike's trying to say," Matt said to the group, "is that the serenity of morning meditation is more useful than a glazed donut."

"Or a honey bun," said Timmy.

Prayer works

Reggie had just returned from a weekend trip to visit his family. It was Sunday evening and he was eager to report his adventures to us as we sat in the breezeway drinking coffee.

"It was a beautiful day when I came out of an AA noon-day meeting," he said. "My plan was to walk down the street to my favorite deli and grab a couple of sandwiches to take home. I was in a sweet, serene state of mind, which made what happened next all the more surprising."

"Go on," said Mike. "We're listening."

Reggie grinned sheepishly and said, "As I was walking, I heard a voice come over my right shoulder. 'You can have a glass of wine while you wait,' it said. I don't have to tell you I was shaken by the thought. They won't be able to smell it on your breath,'"said the voice.

"Well, I know that you can smell wine on anyone's breath. But if the voice said it, I thought, it must be true."

"Woe unto thee, drunkard!" said Robert.

"I knew I was in deep trouble. I was alone, with no one I could reach out to. I'd just come from a meeting, so that wouldn't help. I had no Big Book with me to read and no cell phone to call my sponsor. I was more than a little worried, since one glass of wine would inevitably lead to many, many more before the deli closed at midnight. They would pour me into a taxi, and I would have to face the pained and disappointed looks of my family. Not only that, but I would have to pick up another white chip, and they would almost certainly be sent back to detox. What should I do? Then the voice spoke again."

"Holy shit," said Robert.

"It said, 'You can have two!' Now I was really scared. I knew I was in trouble, but I had absolutely no idea what to do. Then it came to me—I would pray. The only prayer I could think of was the serenity prayer, so I used it. 'God grant me the serenity to accept the things I cannot change, the courage to change the things I can, and the wisdom to know the difference."

"Wow," I said.

"I was so frightened I started praying again. Halfway through I stopped because I couldn't remember why I was praying. I walked into the deli and ordered my sandwiches. It wasn't until later when I paid the bill that I remembered what had happened on the street. I laughed and went home."

Amazing Grace

We were attending a large AA retreat near Lake Lanier. The room was packed but I found a seat near the aisle. The speaker was discussing meditation.

"Sit up straight, put your feet flat on the floor, and close your eyes," he said. "Now, breathe in through your nose and out through your mouth. Don't freak out, but I'm going to turn the lights out."

More than three hundred drunks and junkies became silent in the darkness.

"Now," he said, "I'm going to put on some music."

The refrain was familiar, but I was still taken aback when I remembered the words, "Amazing Grace, how sweet the sound that saved a wretch like me. I once was lost, but now am found. T'was blind but now I see."

I gasped, for in my addiction I had certainly been as lost and blind as a person can be. Then something strange and wonderful happened.

I spoke about it with Mike later that night. "I've known Amazing Grace since I was a kid. My parents would take me to little churches in the wildwood where they played it at every service. My dad would play it on the guitar at Sunday family gatherings. When I learned to play the guitar, I played it myself."

"I can't remember the first time I heard it," said Mike.

"While I was meditating, something amazing happened. I've been afraid to tell anyone."

"Should I call for the priest?" he teased.

"Actually, I did think about seeing Father Mick." I looked straight at Mike. "I was trying to focus my mind on a little spot of light just off the tip of my nose. For a moment, my mind was still and clear. Suddenly my consciousness was filled with an overwhelming white light that expanded until it filled every corner of my mind."

"Holy cow! Were you scared?"

"Sir, I was sore afraid. Too scared to breathe."

"What happened next?" Mike's eyes were wide.

"I held my breath, afraid to move. The light was cool, white, and gentle."

"You're starting to scare me."

"When the music ended, the light vanished instantly. Still afraid to move, I began to take stock of myself. It was then I realized that something incredible had taken place."

"Don't stop," said Mike.

"My younger brother died of leukemia when I was fifteen, and it really shook me up."

"I remember when you shared that in group."

"It was a long time ago, but it's haunted me ever since. When we buried him, I knew I didn't believe in the religion I'd been taught. I could only imagine that in dying, my consciousness would vanish like pulling the plug on a TV set, slipping into an empty oblivion. Anyway, the concept of death as oblivion followed me all during my growing up and into my adult life. The idea of a personal death was a small silent fear that never went away." I paused.

"When the light vanished, I sat very still. Then it hit me. I was no longer afraid of dying. My fear of death had been taken away. For the first time in my adult life, I could take a deep breath without a knot of fear in my belly."

"I see why you haven't told anybody. My mother would have called that the grace of God. She said grace was an unexpected and undeserved gift from God. Sounds like you got a double dose."

"My mom called it the peace that passeth understanding."

"There you go again, trying to turn me into a Christian." He grinned.

"Spiritual truth is where you find it," I said, "whatever the source."

St Francis' Prayer

"Hey, dudes," said Mike, slapping Timmy on the shoulder. "The weather's nice today. Let's go outside and get some fresh air."

"You mean, go outside and smoke a cigarette," said Timmy.

"Maybe we can find some peace under a shady tree," said Robert. "Shall we go?"

With a chorus of spiritual grumbling, we rose as one, dumped our lunch garbage on the way out the door, and headed for the smoking patio. Reggie, our southern-fried preacher from Memphis, was already there. He had a strange look on his face.

"What's on your mind, dude?" asked Mike.

Reggie held up a printed page.

"I've been really down on myself lately," he said.

"Do tell," I said.

"I told my congregation that I walked with the Lord," said Reggie, "but I was lying. The more I preached about a loving God, the more I felt like a hypocrite. I reached a point where I was sure that God had abandoned me. I started isolating. I hid from my flock, avoided my friends and family, and quit answering phone calls. Pretty soon alcohol became my only friend. Jack Daniels was my father confessor. I fell deep into the bottle and didn't care if I ever got out." He closed his eyes for a moment. "But this morning Father Mick gave me this."

He looked down at the paper in his hand and read aloud.

Lord, make me a channel of thy peace,

That where there is hatred, I may bring love;

That where there is wrong, I may bring thy spirit of forgiveness;

That where there is discord, I may bring harmony;

That where there is error, I may bring truth;

That where there is doubt, I may bring faith;

That where there is despair, I may bring hope;

That where there are shadows, I may bring light;

That where there is sadness, I may bring joy.

Lord, grant that I may seek rather to comfort than to be comforted;

To understand, than to be understood;

To love, than to be loved.

For it is by self-forgetting that one finds.

It is by forgiving that one is forgiven.

It is by dying that one awakens to Eternal Life.

"St. Francis's prayer," whispered Robert into my ear.

"Francis of Assisi?" I asked, and Robert nodded.

Reggie gave me his copy of the prayer. I folded it carefully and put it in my pocket

Prayer and Meditation

A total surprise was that prayer worked and was a useful tool in everyday life.

Meditation and prayer are parts of the same experience of touching the divinity within us.

Prayer is a skill that improves with practice. Our state of mind is key to success in prayer.

Morning meditation and prayer centers us for the rest of the day.

They said that AA would take away our fear of death, and it did!

The Prayer of St. Francis provides a useful place to learn about prayer and how we wanted to live.

Prayer is the out-picturing of our heart into the ether.

HIGHER POWER

*"Know that success and inner peace are your birthright,
that you are a child of God and as such that
you're entitled to a life filled with joy, love and happiness."*
—*Wayne Dyer*

There is a God and it ain't you

Giancarlo was the new fish in Timmy's apartment across the way. He was a family practitioner from San Juan and Timmy escorted him to our apartment for community dinner. Giancarlo's ideas about life were about to be shaken.

"Attention! Attention!" Timmy laughed and the guys gathered around. "Giancarlo's from Puerto Rico and I think he's one of us."

John came from his bedroom wearing only gym shorts and tennis shoes. He twirled his tennis racket then adroitly threw it up in the air and caught it.

"Hello, new fish," he said. "First day in rehab." John looked at him sideways. "Well, your first lesson here, is that there is a God, and it ain't you!"

Giancarlo's eyes opened wide. "I...I...Whoa! How did you know? I mean, back home, they treat me like a god, or at least some kind of saint. How did you know?"

The guys all busted out laughing.

"Welcome home," said Timmy.

"This God stuff is kinda sticking in my craw. Always has," I told Cameron during our family therapy session. We were meeting in her small office just off the main hallway.

In detox, large banners listing the Steps and Traditions of Alcoholics Anonymous were hung on the wall. I remember the references to God, but I chose to ignore that part. Now, to get my disease under control and get my medical license back, I was being pushed to give up a lifetime of skepticism.

"I'm assuming that you reached a point where it was either quit or die, right?" she said.

I nodded, wishing I could forget the last horrible days of my using.

"But you didn't have enough power to quit," she said.

Again, I nodded, recalling the uncontrollable impulse to put a needle in my arm.

"And nowhere could you find anything capable of saving you?" she continued.

I wasn't sure where she was going with this.

"I'm sure there must be people who can lick this thing by themselves," she said. "But I don't know any. They say that for us real drunks and junkies, drinking and using were just the symptoms of our underlying insanity. To thrive, or even survive, we must change our way of looking at the world and find a set of spiritual principles that can guide our behavior. To do this requires ...what?"

"Finding a sponsor, working the Steps, and going to meetings," I paused, repeating the catechism. "And learning to pray. But, hey, I've not believed in a personal God in a very long time.

"But I suspect that somewhere, deep inside you, is a concept of God as you think he ought to be," she said. "Not the ideas that were shoved down your throat a kid. Start with that and see where it gets you"

My resistance to my Baptist upbringing had never completely faded. But I knew something was badly wrong with life as I was living it, and I had no idea how to fix it.

Father Mick was addressing the morning session. It was a required session and all the clients in the center were there.

"In the depths of our addiction," he said, "we were sure that God had abandoned us. He was never there when we needed him. He never answered our prayers and he didn't seem to care a whit about us. So, we abandoned the religion of our fathers. It just didn't work for us."

He surveyed the hundred or so faces in the auditorium.

"In the absence of inspiration and guidance, we turned to our own intelligence and self-determination. We knew we could handle this thing called life without help from anyone. But we encountered a world of pain that filled our hearts with fear. In time, we found ourselves alone in the darkness and we cursed the light."

"We found refuge in the bottle and the pipe. None of us woke up one day and decided to become an alcoholic or an addict. Somehow it just happened. We discovered that our using took away our problems and our pain. For me, John Barleycorn became my Higher Power."

"I don't have to remind you of our fall from grace," he said. "We lost everything we valued. Morally bankrupt, living a lie and wishing for death, something happened. Something happened and we ended up here."

"It's been over four years since I walked through the doors of Taylor Rehab Center. Here, they held my hand and told me everything would be alright. I just needed to live by a few spiritual principles. But most of all, they said, I needed to find a God of my own understanding. Because, when push came to shove, when the unstoppable craving for using came over me again, I wouldn't be able to resist. Only with help from a Higher Power would I survive."

"What was it like?" asked Mike. We were riding in a van with two other guys to an AA meeting in north Atlanta. Trying to negotiate eight lanes of Atlanta freeway, he asked, "You know, practicing medicine in a small town? How many docs were there?"

"About fifty," I said.

"So, you must have gone straight to the top of the social register," said Robert from the back seat.

"Boy, I'll say," I said. "You can't do anything at lunch but it's all around town by dinner. I hated it."

"Not like the anonymity of the big city?" asked Mike.

I shook my head. "No, not at all. And the whole thing fed into my sense of superiority. It fanned my arrogance."

"Where was God in all this?" asked Robert. "Was he on the hospital board? Attend any medical society meetings?"

I laughed. "The practice of medicine *was* God. Somehow that slid into the practice of making money. I never had much experience with greed, but I learned fast. In time, I became interested only in how much money I could make off a patient. I skillfully forgot every altruistic motive that propelled me through medical school and house staff training. I focused only on how much money I could make and how fast I could spend it."

I tried not to look like I was about to cry.

"Not much talk of spirituality in the ER, I guess," said Robert after a pause.

I shook my head glumly. "It was easier to discuss your mistress than matters of the heart. In the end, fine wine and powder cocaine became everything to me. I thought about them all the time. I guess you could say that they were my Higher Power."

"Sounds vaguely familiar," Mike said, grinning. "Obviously you need a new Higher Power."

I laughed, but I was terribly afraid of the God I might find.

What is spirituality?

We invited Father Mick out to a Saturday dinner so we could pick his brains about the concept of spirituality.

"There's something inside me, inside all of us, I believe," he began, "some little piece of God. Call it Love, The Holy Ghost, the Christ within, whatever you're comfortable with. Personally, I like the word spirit. I believe this is where my concept of right and wrong live, that it's the source of my virtues. My creativity comes from there, you know, playing the piano, writing poems, that kinda stuff. Like a river, it flows through me and out into the world as love for my fellows."

"Is spirit my Higher Power then?" asked Timmy.

"If it is," I asked, "then how do I relate to him?"

"That's my definition of spirituality," said the priest.

"What is my relationship to God?" asked Robert, reaching for the last of the tortilla chips.

"That would define my moral values, wouldn't it?" said Leon.

"What about conscience?" I asked. "How does that fit in?"

Robert swallowed and said, "'Labor to keep alive in your breast that little spark of celestial fire, called conscience.' George Washington said that." Robert was quoting again.

The waitress arrived with a tray of delightful aromas and began passing plates around.

"And I can tap into this, this force, as it flows through me," said Timmy. "Didn't I hear you say that in morning spiritual?"

Father Mick nodded. "I think love is constantly flowing, from the universe, into me, out to those around me, then back to God. And I can tap into this energy," said Father Mick. "I can use this goodness to guide my thoughts and actions. Hopefully find the life that's promised to me."

"Happy, joyous, and free of fear," said Timmy, his mouth full of food. We fell into quiet meditative eating. Later, as the sopapillas were making their way around, the conversation started up again.

"Can you prove that God exists?" asked Timmy.

"I don't think that you can prove the existence of spiritual things, the way you can prove a theorem in science," said Father Mick. "Science, my doctor friends tell me, is the art of measuring things. But you can't measure ideas like courage or compassion or honesty."

"I've always been a big believer in science," I said, on familiar ground.

"But how did you answer the questions that science rejected?" asked Mike. "Questions that begin with the word 'why'?"

"Mostly I didn't, I guess," I said. I thought for a moment, then said, "That sounds kinda materialistic, doesn't it?"

"More than a little," said Mike. "I think this life"—he waved his arms around as if trying to encompass the universe— "is more than what we see in front of us."

"I don't get it," I said. "How can I know a truth that can't be measured?"

"Well now, that's the point, isn't it?" said Mike.

We fell silent, finished our dinner, and headed home. I had a lot to think about.

It was Sunday evening, and as usual, John was driving fast. We swung from one side of the Atlanta freeway to the other until he found the exit he wanted and slowed down. We pulled up outside the AA meeting house and got out. We were early, so we stood around outside.

"I'm having trouble separating spirituality from religion," I said. What seemed so clear the night before was less so in the light of day.

"If I get up every morning at 7 am and brush my teeth for exactly two minutes and never miss a day," said Robert, "I'm doing it religiously."

"Okay," I said.

"But that's not going to get me sober," he continued. "It's not going to put my life on a spiritual basis."

"Just doing something religiously won't help," said Mike.

"Some guys come into rehab with the idea that their religion is going to save them, and they don't need all this AA stuff," said Robert, who laughed. "So, I like to remind them that their religion didn't keep them from getting drunk in the first place and it certainly didn't get them sober."

"I was raised orthodox," said Leon. "But by the time my alcoholism had swallowed me whole, all my religious upbringing had gone under the bridge."

Robert opened the door to the meeting house. As I passed inside, he whispered to me, "There's more under Heaven and Earth than is dreamt of in your philosophy."

As I passed through the door, I thought, God help me.

God as I understand him

When we returned from the meeting, I opened the Big Book and read the Third Step, "Made a decision to turn our will and our lives over to the care of God as we understood Him." I closed the book slowly and put it down. Mike turned off the TV and put on another pot of coffee. It was already late, but he knew we'd be up for a while.

"I still don't get this part about God, as we understand him," I said.

Robert nodded, "Growing up, I had a lot of trouble with my father's religion, so I dumped it. And God, too. God is dead, they said. It was very cool back then, saying God is dead."

I remembered saying that.

I concentrated on school, worked hard, and kept my head down," said Robert. "The idea of becoming a doctor like my dad kept me grinding away. Respect, status, money—these were all worthy objects to pursue. Especially the respect."

"That low self-esteem thing," said Mike.

"Yeah, but at the time, I thought I was just my altruism."

"How did that work for you?" I asked.

"Not well." said Robert.

Timmy poured himself a cup of coffee and sat beside me on the couch.

"As our lives collapsed, so did our morals," said Mike.

"There were so many things wrong with the image of God they threw at me," I said. "I couldn't swallow all their smug judgmental arrogance."

"I know what you mean," said Reggie. "At times I was embarrassed at the words coming out of my mouth."

We all nodded and fell silent. Our eyes were toward the floor, but we weren't praying. Then Reggie spoke.

"Well, then," he said, "let's clear out our old ideas and start from scratch? Who wants to go first?"

Timmy raised his hand. I carefully brought it down again. "Unconditional love," he said.

"What?" I asked.

"I don't know," said Timmy, "it just popped into my head. I'm not even sure what it means."

Leon raised his eyes. "It means just that, love without conditions. I will love you whether you love me or not."

"I love you for the God inside you," said Reggie. "I'll never stop loving you, no matter what you say or do."

"And I want nothing in return," said Robert, "no quid pro quo."

"Kinda like my dog," said Timmy. "She'll love me even if I forget her birthday or our anniversary." He giggled.

"No matter what sin I commit," said Leon, "this Higher Power will not withhold his forgiveness."

"That must mean he's willing to forgive everything," I said. "Surely you can't mean that."

"That's exactly what I do mean," said Leon.

"I think I'm getting it," said Timmy.

"God made me, and he knows exactly what I'm capable of," said Robert. "He knows how I'll respond in any situation and he'll forgive me when I make the wrong choice. That doesn't mean that I can commit an endless series of sins and expect forgiveness over and over. That's not how forgiveness works. Which brings me to another point. My God doesn't test me. He doesn't try to trick me into making a mistake. I'm quite capable of making mistakes all by myself."

"God is not mocked," said Timmy, "and he doesn't mock his children."

"And God doesn't punish us," said Reggie. "We do a good enough job punishing ourselves without any help from the Almighty."

I was still holding back. "But I'm having trouble with the word God. It conjures up all the revulsion I felt for the self-righteous salesmen of organized religion. Just the word itself makes me recoil."

"That's why they chose the words Higher Power," said Leon. It has to be *your* conception of a God. Something you can relate to and reach out to when you need help."

"We're all children of God," said Reggie slowly, as if chewing on the words, "all his sons and daughters, all equal in his sight. No one is better or worse than anyone else."

"That's why the Lord's Prayer begins with the words Our Father," I thought out loud.

"Sometimes I think of God as the benevolent uncle," said Robert.

"Like Walter Cronkite?" asked Timmy.

"Avuncular," I nodded.

"Uncle God will never interfere with my life," said Robert. "He's too kind and polite. After all, he gave us free will, didn't he?"

Timmy and I both nodded.

"He'll keep hands off until we ask him," Robert said, "but he'll always respond if we ask. He's very good that way."

"Don't stop now," said Timmy.

"Okay, you asked for it," said Robert. "God is not up in the sky sitting on some exalted throne. God is here. Right here, right now. There is nowhere I can go where God is not, for all of God's creation exists within him. Nothing can exist outside God, including me."

"So, I'm within God," I said, trying to wrap my head around this new idea. Somehow, I think I already knew that."

"And God is within me," said Timmy. "That's comforting."

"Yes, yes," I said, "that makes sense. I must look for God, not outside, but inside."

"And if he's within me," Robert said, grinning, "then God is always accessible to me. I don't need a priest or rabbi to interpret for me."

"If I knock on the door, he'll answer," I said.

"Cool," said Timmy.

"And if he's inside me, then only I can block the light of his love," said Robert.

"Careful," I said, "You're starting to sound like Stephen."

"And God can touch me anytime," said Timmy, smiling his ass off. "God can touch me with a moment of clarity or a white light, or ….whatever."

Or even a simple new understanding, I thought.

I walked outside and sat by myself in the moonlight. This thought suddenly appeared in my head: If God is unconditional love, then, by definition, life is good. Maybe it's true after all, that life is supposed to be easy. Maybe.

How do I love something I can't see?

I was sitting in the back row of an AA meeting in Buckhead, lost in thought.

I wanted to believe in something, but the sound of the evangelist's words in my ears still made me cringe. I am the one responsible for all the successes in my life, I thought. I control my own destiny. My head might be bloody, but it was definitely unbowed. Then I looked around at a room filled with people who had thought the same thing. Maybe I wasn't an alcoholic after all. I'm not like these people. Maybe I didn't have this stupid disease. If I could just get out of here, I was sure I could lick this thing on my own.

I looked over at Mike sitting next to me. As if reading my thoughts, he said, "Your ego is killing you." The next day I made an appointment to see Father Mick.

It was after lunch and I was getting sleepy, so I was glad to smell freshly brewed coffee when the good Father opened his door. I was surprised at the first question that came out of my mouth.

"How do I love something I can't see?" I said.

He paused thoughtfully while he stuffed fresh tobacco into his pipe.

"You could begin by loving those things you *can* see," he said. "Expressions of a Higher Power you see every day."

"Like sunsets, you mean?" I asked.

"Or flowers," he said. "Or smiles on the faces of small children."

"Butterflies and puppies, especially puppies." I grinned. "Or acts of kindness to strangers,"

"The stars at night," said the priest. "The love that flows through your heart."

Oh, my God, I thought. "You mean other people, too, don't you? To see the presence of God in everyone I meet? That may take some doing."

"You do have a lifetime to get it right," he said.

"But, Father Mick," I said. "I'm still having trouble with all the terrible things that have been done in his name."

"We don't have to concern ourselves today with man's inhumanity to man," he said, lighting his pipe. "We're just concerned with our journey through this life, yours and mine. You see, every person has their own path to walk. Each of us must find our own conception of a Higher Power."

His pipe went out and he lit it again.

"When you reach your first approximation of the God-of-your-understanding, the word God will take on a new meaning. When you say, 'God,' you will mean your God, not anyone else's."

"First approximation?" I asked.

"Yes, you see, finding a Higher Power is a process, not an event," he said. "Don't expect a burning bush to jump out in front of you. As you continue to grow spiritually, so will your ideas about God."

I sighed, half excited to begin yet still frightened at what I might find. "How do I begin?"

"Ego deflation," he said. When I arrived in detox, my ego was so wildly out of control that there was no room for a God of any kind. My ability to turn my will over to God is inversely proportional to the size of my ego."

Your ego is killing you; I heard Mike's words echoing in my mind.

I know there is a God

I was surprised when I got the card from my oldest daughter. They claimed that the rehab center was off the radar, and no one was supposed to know where I was.

I smiled and opened it. On the front it read, "Once Carl Jung was asked if he believed there was a God". I opened the card. Inside was his answer, "Sir," said Jung, "I do not believe there is a God. I know there is a God!"

Higher Power

Our first lesson in rehab: "There is a God and it ain't you."

We had abandoned our old ideas about a Higher Power and instead worshipped at the altar of our drug of choice.

Deep inside each of us was the idea of some power greater than ourselves.

Finding a Higher Power that could help us live a better life is a process, not an event.

Spirituality can be defined as how we relate to the universe and how we behave in this world based on that relationship.

Spiritual values such as honesty, kindness, and compassion, can be experienced but not measured.

We could see the Higher Power of our understanding in the world around us, in sunsets, flowers, and the faces of others.

A New Way of Thinking

"The world we see that seems so insane is the result of a belief system that is not working. To perceive the world differently, we must be willing to change our belief system, let the past slip away, expand our sense of now, and dissolve the fear in our minds."
—William James

Who am I?

I sucked down the last of my coffee, threw the cup in the trash, and took my seat in Matt's morning session. I had taken to sitting up front. The recovery was better up there, I'd been told.

"Everything you think you know about living is wrong," said Matt. "I know you've heard that before. Nonetheless it's true. Which means you have to throw out all your old ways of thinking and start your lives over again."

I swear he was staring straight at me. I blinked.

"That's simply another way of saying that you have to take stock of who you are and why you're in this world. What are the most important things in your life, if they're not drugs and alcohol?"

Matt was definitely looking at me. I blinked again.

"You need new priorities, don't you Lin?" he said.

I nodded.

"In your old life, when you thought you were king of the world, what were your top three priorities?"

I didn't have to think long before I answered. "My job, my job, my job."

Matt nodded. "What about family? What about God?"

"I'm sure my family was on the list somewhere," I peeped, "but I'm not sure God made the cut."

"So, you will be making a new list now,?" he asked.

"Right," I answered.

"Now for the question of the day," he said. "Who are you?"

"I'm an oncologist," I said proudly, hoping to gain a few points. But Matt said, "No that's what you used to do. Try again."

"Uh, I'm a father and a husband," I said, hoping it would appease my counselor.

Matt shook his head. "No-o-o, those are your relationships."

I was stumped. My old ideas about who I was, were circling the drain, going down fast. I scrambled for an answer that I knew would be wrong.

"Uh, I'm a flattop guitar picker from Tennessee?"

Matt just shook his head and sighed.

A Child of God

Robert caught me in the hallway between sessions, put his arm around my shoulders, and pulled me into an empty classroom. He inspected the room to make sure it was empty, then shut the door behind us.

"Today in group," he said, "Matt asked 'Who are you?'"

I nodded and started mumbling something about the unfairness of life when Robert put his hand over my mouth.

"If you'll shut up for one minute," he said, "I'll tell you."

"Please," I mumbled between his fingers.

"You're a child of God," he said, "and your job—the reason you're alive today—is to bring God's love into the world. You were not put on this earth to sell shoes, make bricks, or write prescriptions. Not to climb the corporate ladder, run for political office, nor accumulate the most toys."

Robert stared at me so solemnly I was afraid to say anything.

"On the lighter side," he said smiling broadly, "it's time for lunch. Come on."

Later the same day, Cameron was talking about her relationship with a Higher Power.

"When I started working on my concept of a Higher Power," she began, "I remembered the words my mother told me long ago. That I was more than just my body. That my relationship to God was that of parent to child. That his will for me was not *what* I was supposed to do, but *how* I was supposed to live."

I immediately thought about what Robert had said. Then it dawned on me. There was a basic truth here, although I couldn't put it into words—a recognition of something I had known before, but somehow I had forgotten. The remembering sent an indescribably warm feeling through me. I had thrown out all the trappings of religion without realizing that I might have thrown out the good stuff as well. Something was stirring within me.

Cameron continued. "In many AA meetings, we close with the Lord's Prayer. What are the first two words of the prayer?"

"Our Father," said several people almost as one.

"Yes," smiled Cameron. "Yes. And if God is our parent, then we are his children.

"We're made in His image!" said Timmy, sitting beside me. "Wow!"

"What does it mean to be a child of God?" I asked, trying to fit the pieces of the puzzle together.

"Maybe you can answer your own question," she said.

The words came tumbling out. "If my Higher Power is unconditional love, then I am a creature made of that same love," I said.

"Go on," said Cameron.

"I partake of all of his good qualities," I said.

"So, I'm a good person with a bad disease," said Timmy, almost beside himself.

"And what about the power I need to defend me when I'm overwhelmed by the thought of picking up a drink?" asked Cameron.

"A power greater than myself," said Timmy. "Whoa!"

"I was hopeless when I got here," I said, "Life was a blackness with no hope at all. Nothing good would ever happen in my life again." I paused as the thoughts formed. "I can still sense that terrible…desperation…moving inside my head."

"'I once was lost, but now I'm found, was blind, but now I see,'" quoted The Robert.

"I'll never have perfect goodness, in either my body or my mind," said Leon, "but the divinity within me *is* perfect. The goal of recovery is to let this goodness, my goodness, out into the world."

"I believe this means," said Cameron, "that we're all honest, loving, and caring people—and most importantly—worthy of the love and respect of others. We truly are the children of God."

I wrapped my arms around this idea, for it filled some hole in my heart that needed filling.

God provides

Robert and I went to see Father Mick. We were wrestling with a problem we couldn't solve.

I went first. "I'm still struggling to find a Higher Power that I can relate to. I want to believe in a power greater than myself and all, but I guess I'm having trouble reconciling these new ideas with my career-driven world."

"The world is too much with us; late and soon, getting and spending, we lay waste our powers," quoted Robert. "Wordsworth."

"I feel trapped in the world of Caesar," I said. "My self-worth has always been tied to how much money I made and my position in society. I'm afraid of what tomorrow will bring, deathly afraid that I won't make as much money as I used to."

"This way of thinking leaves you living in fear, doesn't it?" asked Father Mick.

"I know, Father Mick," said Robert. "I know in my head that all good things come from God, but I'm having trouble letting go of the idea that I'm the one that earns my money and I alone am responsible for my life."

"Are you responsible for the sun?" asked Father Mick. "Without the sun to provide heat and light, there'd be no plant life, no animals, and no humans. What good would your paycheck be then?"

"Yes, but ..." I said and fell silent.

"It's God that provides. He gives you the health and intelligence to work and to earn. It's not a meaningless platitude to say 'All good things come from God.' He provides for the birds of the air and the lilies of the field, and they certainly don't work a 40-hour week. And just as you, the imperfect parent, want to provide good things for your children, so the God of your understanding wants to provide for you. You just have to give him the chance."

Father Mick smiled at us both, and I withered under the love in his gaze.

"I could ask you the question that God posed to Job," he said softly.

"Which was?" asked Robert.

"Where were you when I laid the foundations of the earth?" said Father Mick. "Declare, if you have understanding."

Daily Bread

This was Cameron's last session. She was taking a position with a treatment center near her mother's home in New England. Her mother was sick and probably dying. Since Cameron had no real attachments in the Atlanta area, she was leaving us.

"For our last session," she began, "I'd like for us to talk about daily bread. Who can tell me what daily bread is?"

After a moment, Mike answered. "It's a line from the Lord's Prayer. You know, where we ask God to feed us today."

"Good," said Cameron.

"Like the manna God showered on the children of Israel when they were lost in the desert." said Leon. "That manna was only good for a single day."

"Better," she said, smiling. "And what is daily bread besides food?" she asked. The morning sunlight coming through the window was radiant on her face.

"What we need to survive each day," said Robert.

"Yes," said Cameron. "Spiritually, bread is a metaphor for all the needs we require on any given day. Not just the material things, like food, shelter, and clothing, but also those things that nurture the spirit, like fellowship, love, and serenity. And we need these things every day. We can't eat once a month and be filled."

"At a meeting last week, the speaker said he had the disease of addiction," said Timmy. "He said he treated his disease with a daily dose of spirituality, and he got this spirituality from prayer and meditation, and from going to AA meetings. I guess that might be daily bread."

"Very good, my Timmy. And from what well do these gifts spring?"

"God is supposed to provide for us, isn't he?" asked Mike.

"But don't go in a closet, shut the door," said Robert, "then tell God you're hungry and expect a hot dog to come rolling under the door," said Robert. "It doesn't work like that."

"No, it doesn't," said Cameron. "You have to claim your daily bread. You must recognize and know in your heart that God is the source of all goodness. If I believe in lack, I'll be left wanting. If I believe that God is the source of all the good things in my life and claim that goodness, I'll never lack."

"What else?" asked Timmy, softly.

"I'll miss your gentle heart, my Timmy," said Cameron. "Yes, there is one more thing. Knowing that God provides is not enough. What's required is an actual realization, a vibrant living of that faith."

Timmy looked puzzled.

"Just looking at a plate of food does me no good," she continued. "If I give lectures on the benefits of food or write poems to its great nutritional value, I'm not sustained. Singing songs of praise to bread won't nourish my body. No one can chew the food and swallow it for me. I must eat the food myself and incorporate it into my being. And the process is good for only one day. Tomorrow I must do it again."

"Daily bread, with butter?" asked Timmy.

"Yes, Timmy." She folded her hands in front of her as her gaze moved from face to face. "Namaste. God bless you all," she said.

Desire comes from God

Jane stood at the front of the class, her arms crossed. Her jaw seemed more pointed than usual and her eyes were sharp as knives.

"Where does desire come from?" she asked pointedly.

"From the devil?" asked Timmy.

"But doesn't that eliminate my part in my mistakes, and let me avoid the consequences of my actions?" She looked in Robert's direction.

"We've come to believe that we alone are responsible for our problems," he answered.

"And …?" asked Jane.

The room was quiet.

"All desire comes from God," she said.

"But …" Timmy sputtered.

"Repeat after me, class," she said. She intoned, "All desire comes from God."

We dutifully responded, "All desire comes from God."

"Then our mistakes must come from twisting that desire into a less than useful direction," said Robert, thinking out loud.

"Precisely," said Jane. "Free will is sometimes a curse, since it lets us pursue actions that are harmful. As alcoholics and addicts, our feeble minds may ofttimes lead us astray."

"I have a broken thinker," said Robert. "I need all the help I can get making decisions in the material world."

"And where can I find such help?" asked Jane.

"From my sponsor," said Timmy.

"From my psychiatrist and my counselor," said Mike.

"Where else?" Jane asked.

"From the fellowship in AA meetings," said Timmy.

"From my Higher Power," whispered Reggie.

"Good," said Jane, "and how do I handle the desires I've twisted into harmfulness?"

Again, the room fell silent. After a few moments, Jane smiled.

"First, I need to recognize that the object of my desire is harmful."

"Desire for women is a big problem for me," said Timmy.

"Mine too—especially the ones who sit in the front row," said Reggie.

"My desire to look good in public," I mumbled.

"This next part is really important," she said. "You'll need to return to God the desire he has given you. Let your desire focus on God and his love. You can ask him to help you change the direction of your cravings, away from a passion for the world, and into a passion for serenity and a relationship with him. Every time a useless appetite arises within you, whatever its object, first recognize its nature, then convert that craving into love and send that love back home to God."

Timmy spoke, "God, take away my lust for women and the other thing she said."

Whose car is it?

Saturday morning, we piled into the van. It was shopping and haircut day and we went as a group. John wiped the sleep from his eyes and cranked up the engine.

"First stop," he shouted, "coffee!" We all cheered.

Next to John up front was Wee Willy, who lately seemed a wee bit of a different man. Round Robert and I took the first-row seat while Reggie took the back seat with my buddy Mike.

"Who was at Stan's NA meeting last night?" asked Wee Willy.

"I was chasing Little Susie around the parking lot," Mike bragged.

"Liar, liar, pants on fire," said Robert.

"I was the one sleeping in the back," said John.

"Did you hear Stan rip into our pal here?" asked Wee Willy, staring straight at me. I blushed as I recalled the grilling Stan had given me.

"Do tell," asked Mike.

"He asked Lin whose car he was driving," said Robert. "Buddy boy made the mistake of saying it was his." He laughed.

"Come on, guys," I said. He set me up. He sees me as a good example of how not to think."

"Yup," said Robert. "Got that right."

"So, what'd Stan say?" asked Mike.

"Stan most pointedly told me it was God's car," I said. "He told me I'd better take care of it because I have to give it back every night."

"Gotcha there," said Reggie, starting to wake up.

"I'm very proud of my shiny new car, and I didn't like Stan saying that it wasn't mine," I said. "I don't remember God standing around the driveway to take my car back every evening."

"I'm not sure God has been in your life at all lately," said Reggie.

"I didn't like the way the conversation was going," I said. "It didn't make sense to me. Then he started in on my house and I had a sudden sinking feeling that he might be right. Stan's idea about God was the owner had never occurred to me. After all, I'd earned the money to buy the land and build the house."

"Yes," said Robert. "We've all heard about your wonderful house."

"By then I was starting to get the idea," I said, "so I told Stan it was God's house and I'd better take care of it because I had to give it back every night. I must admit, I wasn't too hot about this new way of thinking about my material possessions."

"I kinda like the idea," said Reggie. "It is God's world, not mine."

"Then, one of Stan's students spoke up and asked him about the money in our bank accounts," I said. "The student asked, whose is that?"

"Stan said it belonged to God," said Robert. "He said, when the money belonged to Stan, people came out of the woodwork trying to take it away from him. He went around hoarding money, always trying to get more, afraid he'd never have enough."

"Greed," said Reggie. "The love of money is the root of evil and all."

"Stan said, now he knows the money belongs to God," Robert continued, "and his job is to be a steward of the money, putting it where it does the most good, distributing it into the right pockets. He doesn't worry anymore about how much money he has. It'll always be replaced when more is needed."

Our first stop was at Caribou Café for the day's first dose of caffeine. There was an immediate improvement in the group's attitude.

"What about children?" asked John, settling back into the van with his coffee. "I have two kids. Do they belong to God too?"

"You could certainly argue that our children belong to God," said Mike. "If my car, my house, and my money belong to God then I would think my kids belong to him as well. After all, who knows my child's heart better than God? And who can provide for them better than God?"

"In Genesis," said Reggie, "God tells Abraham to take his son Isaac and offer him as a burnt offering. This sounds horribly barbaric. As you've said, Mike, we love our children more than anything else."

"Even ahead of our Higher Power?" asked Wee Willy. "Isn't that like worshiping a false idol, having another god before him?"

"That's exactly the point," said Reggie. "I'll lose anything I place above my Higher Power. That includes worldly possessions, honors, and certainly children. Our relationship with God must become my highest priority. The love I get from God, I can then shower on my kids. The more I love God, the more I'm able to love my children."

"So, God was teaching Abraham that he must not let his love for Isaac become more important than his love for God," said Wee Willy, smiling. "God never intended for Abraham to harm his son."

This last caused a hush to fall over the group. We arrived at the barbershop.

As I climbed into the barber chair, Wee Willy spoke. "We might as well go the whole hawg," he said. "If this is God's world and not Wee Willy's, then whose life is it?"

"It can only be God's life, not mine," I said. I was going the whole hawg.

"I certainly didn't will myself into existence," said Reggie. "And unless I commit suicide, I won't will myself out of existence."

"I always considered this life to be mine," said Mike. "Mine to screw up or make a success of. Mine to waste or put to good use."

"Our lives are a gift, a most precious and wonderful gift," said Reggie. We have dominion over them, but they don't belong to us. They are given to us to shepherd. Like my car, my house, and my money, my life belongs to God."

"And when I'm done with my body at the end of my time," said Wee Willy, "I have to give it back to God, so I'd better take care of it."

"If I knew I was going to live this long, I would've taken better care of it," said Mike, putting out his cigarette as he got in the car.

A New Way of Thinking

The process of recovery is essentially the process of discovering who I am as a person.

The simplest answer was that "I am a child of the Universe, and my job in this life is to bring the love of the Universe into the world."

We discovered that all of our needs were provided for by the Universe.

Daily bread was the gift of the Universe. We only had to reach out to receive it.

All desire comes from God. It is our ego that perverts desire toward the material life.

The world is God's, not mine. It is his gift to me as his child.

The pursuit of material goods blocks my journey on the spiritual path.

Finding recovery and the serenity it brings provides all the material goods I need.

I Can Control My Thoughts

"There is no thing good or bad,
Except my thinking makes it so."
—*Shakespeare*

I am the source of all my problems

Outside, the approaching fall was coloring the leaves and the sun was thin but inside Matt's morning session, the lights were bright and friendly.

"I must understand that I'm the source of all of my problems. Not God, not fate, not my disease," said Matt. "No ill-tempered winds blow trouble my way. No other person is responsible for my sorrows and heartaches. I alone am the source of my torments."

"It took me forever to realize that my ex-wife and her lawyers were not the cause of my problems," said Mike. "For a long time, I blamed them for every bad thing that happened. If my dog pooped on the rug, it was their fault."

"Didn't you say we had to dump all our blame and shame and guilt?" asked Timmy.

"Yes," said Matt. "How did you overcome your dog's poop?"

"Slowly," Mike said, "and I do mean slowly. As much as I'd like to, I can't change the behavior of others. But I can change my thinking and how I respond to them. You taught me that I alone am responsible for the consequences of my actions."

"Did you blame yourself?" asked Timmy.

"At first," said Mike. "But like Matt said, I can't hold onto blame anymore."

"So, God isn't punishing you?" asked Matt.

"Nope," said Mike. "I'm the only one punishing me."

I have no control over the world

After lunch, we reconvened on the breezeway, awash with the smell of rain on hot pavement. A cool mist floated around us.

"Accepting the world as it is means I have to recognize that I'm not in charge of the world," said Mike. "As much as I'd like to control everything around me, today I know that all the people, places, and things I encounter are well beyond my ability to change them."

"But ..." said Timmy.

"No buts about it," said Robert, who joyfully found a pack of salted peanuts in his pocket. "You have no control over anything in this world."

"What about bodily functions?" asked Wee Willy, a man of podiatric science.

"The next time you have a bad bout of the runs," said Mike, "stand outside the bathroom door and repeat after me: I will not have diarrhea, I will not have diarrhea, and see what happens."

"I certainly don't have control over my pancreas or my pituitary," I said. "Nor can I will myself to grow an extra six inches so I can make the basketball team."

"All right, Mr. Smarty Pants," said Timmy, "what do I have control over?"

"Your thoughts, my good friend," said Robert, quickly gulping down the peanuts. "You have control of only one thing in this life—your thoughts."

John came out from the apartment, "Coffee's ready."

We filled our cups and returned to the breezeway.

"All kinds of terrible ideas come into my head sometimes," said Timmy. "What about them, huh?"

"All manner of thoughts come unbidden to my mind," said Robert, washing down the peanuts with fresh coffee. "Thoughts of punching my neighbor, poisoning his dog, or screwing his old lady, but also thoughts of helping him rake his leaves, bringing him food in times of illness, or giving him a ride when his car's in the shop."

"I'm not responsible for the thoughts that come flying into my head," said Mike. "But I am responsible for what I do with them. I can either reject them—refuse to give them a place in my mind—or I can hold onto them, maybe even obsess on them."

"If I obsess on something," asked Timmy, "won't I draw it to me?"

Later, in Raphael's class...

"One of the secrets of life is this," said Raphael: "whatever I focus my attention on, I draw to me." Raphael was Cameron's replacement. Small framed, with jet black hair and eyes, he was the only Hispanic on staff. We immediately liked him.

"If I focus on a cold beer, pretty soon it'll be in my hand. Being obsessive-compulsive, I'm good at fixating on any thought that passes through my mind. If I hold onto that thought it will eventually become my reality. If I reject the thought, it will have no effect on my world. Once I understand where my freedom lies, I'm the one who gets to choose."

"In other words," said Timmy, "I'm not responsible for the first thought that comes into my head, but I am responsible for what I do with it. If the thought of getting high enters my head, I have the choice of obsessing on it or rejecting it."

"Matt said the way the human mind is constructed, it can only hold one thought at a time," said Reggie, brandishing a lemonade topped with a slice of lime. "By focusing my attention on lemonade, I effectively reject the thought of a cold beer."

"That makes sense," I said.

"It's a good way to fight off negative thoughts," said Raphael. "I can switch my attention to a ball game on TV or where to go for dinner," he said.

"My problem," said Timmy, "is when the thought keeps coming back."

"The only real defense against the first drink comes from my Higher Power," said Reggie. "If the thought of using refuses to leave, I can pray what Cameron taught us:

"God,
I thank you for taking away my obsession with drinking,
and replace it with the faith that no matter what happens,
everything will be alright."

"If I focus on the problem," said Robert, "I'm stuck."

"But if I focus on the solution, I'm free," said Raphael.

Raphael continued. "Last week I was driving downtown and pulled to a stop at a traffic light. An old song by Sting started playing on the radio. My ex-wife and I had partied and gotten high listening to it. In a flash of anger, a flood of resentments against my ex-wife filled my mind and the memory of our marital woes came roaring back. In an instant, I was filled with rage. It mattered not that all this had occurred years before, the hurt seemed as fresh as yesterday. Staring into the traffic light, I knew exactly what I had to do. I closed my eyes and prayed."

"God,
I thank you for taking away my resentment against my ex-wife
and replacing it with the faith that no matter
what happens, everything will be all right."

"Just as quickly as it had arrived, the resentment was gone. The song ended, the light turned green, and I drove off. And I had been spared hours of angry grief and turmoil," said Raphael. "Resentments won't go away by themselves. A song on the radio, a fragrance of perfume, or an old memory can bring about the full-blown explosion of old anger."

"Matt said alcoholics and addicts are especially sensitive to resentments," said Timmy.

"To keep from accumulating new resentments," said Raphael, "I must deal with them the moment they arise. I need to recognize what's happening, forgive the other person right away, and apologize as quickly as possible for my part in the trouble. That way, lingering resentments won't fester until they become nearly impossible to root out."

Forms of Negativity

Matt called the session to order. "Today, we're going to try and improve your stinking thinking. Let's start by naming the forms of negativity that intrude upon your minds. Mike?"

"Dwelling on a past I can't change," he said.

"Good start," said Matt. "What else?"

"Worrying over a future that may never materialize," said Vera.

"Living in fear of any kind?" said Timmy.

"Yes, of course," said Matt, "but let's be a little more specific."

"How about ruminating on what should've been, or what could've been?" Timmy asked.

"Excellent, Timmy," said Matt.

I spoke next. "'What if' and 'if only'."

"All these are good," said Matt, "How about blame and shame and guilt? We've mentioned them before. They will always affect my thinking unless I dump them. They're deadly for the addict and alcoholic."

"Ever since I was a kid, I've blamed myself for all the world's problems," said Vera. "When my father got mad it was always because of me. When my parents divorced, I was sure it was my fault. Today I still beat myself up over my mistakes."

"I know that if you scratch my shame," I said, "you'll get an instant angry response."

"My sins left me with this overwhelming sense of both shame and guilt," said Reggie. "My pain was so great, only my friend Jack Daniels could relieve it."

"Exactly," said Matt. "You need you to dump all your blame and shame and guilt here in this room, and I suggest you start doing it now. If you don't, you'll use again, and if you use again ..."

"We'll die," came the chorus from the room.

Don't act reflexively

We were again in Jane's classroom. For some reason, the high priestess of intimidation was mellow this day. She smiled benignly at Reggie and stuck her pencil into her henna-dyed bun.

Reggie said, "I've been considering what Matt said about changing our thinking. Could you help me with this?"

Jane pursed her lips thoughtfully then placed her ruler on the desk.

"One of the central ideas of AA is that I no longer have to respond blindly to what happens in the world around me," Jane said, glaring when she saw me. "My old thinking consisted of two steps. First, you insult me, then reflexively, I hit you in the nose. Now, I'm no longer have to respond that way. Now it becomes, insult me, and I stop and think, that's interesting, I wonder what he meant by that, and I turn and walk away." She patted the bald spot on the top of my head and said, "We no longer have to respond blindly to the first thought in our head."

"I'm with you," said Reggie. "But how does that help me get rid of all the negativity that lives inside my head?"

"I need to recognize negative thoughts as soon as they arise so I can dispose of them quickly," Jane said. "I need to be constantly on guard for such thoughts."

"Oh Lord," said Reggie, "how long would that take, I wonder?"

"Six months," said our counselor. "It took me six months to go from being full of negativity to a place where it no longer colored my thinking and affected my behavior. I'll never be free of every negative thought, but at least today I can recognize one when it appears and dump it as quickly as possible. Constant vigilance of my thoughts is the price of my serenity."

She looked directly at me. "Of course, for some of you, it may take a little longer."

I Can Control My Thoughts

When we realized that we were the source of all our problems, we quit blaming others.

Despite my struggling, I have no control over the material world.

All I have control over are the thoughts in my head.

I am not responsible for the first thought that pops up in my head. But I am responsible for what I do with that thought.

I must be vigilant of my thoughts if I want to control them.

I must remove negativity in all its forms to find happiness.

Holding onto resentments and judging others is poison to us.

By observing my thoughts as they arise, I no longer have to respond reflexively.

I'm Starting to Wake Up

*"Keep on adding, keep on walking, keep on progressing:
Do not delay on the road, do not go back, do not deviate."*
—*Augustine*

I am responsible for the consequences of my actions

After the last group of the day, Leon and I were asked to take a newcomer named Brice to the apartment and introduce him to the fellows. We escorted him to dinner and an AA meeting then sat in the apartment talking. It was well past bedtime, but Leon and I sat patiently listening to Brice, a lawyer from Memphis, droning on. This was not his first time in rehab, and he was sure he had it all figured out. He trotted out one fine platitude after another.

"I got high a lot of times and never got in trouble, but every time I got in trouble, I was high," he said. "I'm not my disease any more than I'm my arthritis. I'm a good person with a bad disease."

Leon and I nodded in agreement.

"If I were simply a bad person, I'd be without hope for change. If it's my disease that provokes my bad behavior and if my disease can be treated, then there's hope for me."

"And without hope," said Leon, "nothing's possible." I yawned my agreement. Brice seemed very pleased with himself.

Brice yawned. "Time for bed," he said.

Leon almost smirked. "Not quite yet," he said. "I think you forgot something."

Puzzled, Brice asked, "What?"

"Brice," I said. "You are without a doubt the most arrogant drunk I've met all week. Sure, the disease theory explains a lot about the nature of our addiction. But you have conveniently forgotten that you and you alone are responsible for the consequences of your actions. Now we're going to bed."

Jane sat primly on the desk, legs crossed, looking at no one in particular.

"When I was using," she said, "I ignored all the consequences of my drinking—broken family, broken job, broken morals. Denial provided me with effective mental blinders. Mike?"

"I know this much," said Mike. "I would go into a nightclub, sit at the end of the bar, and drink until I closed the place down. To my mind, I wasn't hurting anyone. As far as I was concerned, there were no consequences to my using."

"And now?" said Jane.

"Now I understand how I hurt others. My wife, who never saw me, my kids who only saw me drunk, and my parents, who were glad they never saw me. My performance on the job suffered and my coworkers had to cover for me. The yard went unmowed because I was too hungover. The screen door never got fixed. The list goes on and on and on."

"You were a bad boy," said Jane.

"You are a bad boy," whispered Robert.

"Glynnis?" said Jane.

"I would start smoking crack early Saturday morning," Glynnis began. She was a nurse from Savannah, dedicated to her patients but more dedicated to her cocaine. "The kids wanted my attention, but I was too busy getting high. I told them to go watch TV or play outside on the swings. Anything, just don't interrupt me. I promised myself I would go play with them as soon as I got a good buzz on, but I never did."

"Once I went to visit the dope man in the worst part of the projects. My two-year-old daughter, Laurie, was in the backseat waiting while I went inside—just long enough to buy my dope, I said. Three hours later, wasted and sweaty, I suddenly remembered she was out in the car. When I got to her, she was crying, starving, and scared to death."

"That's frightening," whispered Mike, "but I've done just as bad."

My mind's eye flashed on a scene just before I went to detox. Six women worked in my office, some for years. I had visited their houses, eaten at their tables, written letters of recommendation for their kids, even bailed one out of jail. I called them together and told them I was closing the practice. Marty, my transcriptionist, began to cry. I assumed she was crying for me. Immersed in my own self-pity, I couldn't see any other reason. Marty wiped her eyes, her face a blubbery mess. 'My husband Jimmy's out of work,' she said, 'and I'm afraid we'll lose our house.'

What is my part?

Leon poured himself a cup of coffee and sat down beside me.

"I'm having a bad day," he said. "Really bad." His face looked like sundown in a rainstorm.

"Yes?"

"My wife's getting an abortion." His voice was flat and low.

"What?" I knew Leon and his wife Hannah were separated.

He stared into his coffee. "She found out last week she's pregnant."

"So why …?"

"She's sick and tired of putting up with my bullshit. Of the ten years we've been married I've been wasted for at least nine—ruined birthdays, holidays, anniversaries, every kind of family thing. Spent rent money for drugs, gave her car to the dope man." He raked a hand through his hair, exhaling loudly. "I've been fired from more jobs than you can count. Been in court for drunk driving, bad checks, IRS. Humiliated her in front of her family, in department stores, in temple, for God's sake. And I've demonstrated pretty clearly that I can't be trusted. She finally ran out of patience and she doesn't want to have anything more to do with me."

"And she wants an abortion?"

He looked at his watch. "She had it an hour ago."

"What're you going to do?"

His voice dropped even further. "I was thinking about going over to the 'hood and scoring some heroin. Wanna come along?"

"I think not," I said.

"Right now, I'll do just about anything to make this hurting stop." He buried his face in his hands. "Case of beer and a bottle of vodka?" he mumbled. His red eyes peered at me between his fingers.

"And what'll happen if we do?"

"We both know the answer to that," he said.

"A horrible thing has happened and you have to decide what to do."

"When I was using, I wouldn't have given it a thought. I would've gotten smashed."

"Did that ever make anything better?"

"No."

"What are your options?" I asked. "Today, you can choose how to respond. You can obsess on the thought of using or replace the thought with a better one."

His grimace smoothed out a little. "We could get some ice cream and watch the Knicks."

"That'd be a start."

He grunted and looked up. "We could go to group and I could share how bad I feel."

"That's better. Keep going."

"I could ask the question, what's my part in all this?" said Leon. "What is it about me that's upset? A part of me has been destroyed. I feel betrayed. My pride's hurt. My self-esteem is dashed. Shall I go on?"

"And what's at the bottom of this list of your character defects?"

"Fear," he said. "Hey, didn't we learn a prayer for that?" He closed his eyes and recited:

> *"God, I thank you for taking away my fear*
> *And replacing it with the faith*
> *That no matter what happens,*
> *Everything will be alright.*

"Oh, I just remembered something else," he said. "In everything, there's a lesson and a blessing. But I'll tackle that after two scoops of ice cream."

I can't fix things

The sun was a pale yellow dot in a gray October sky. We were in Matt's morning session discussing how addicts like to fix things.

"The role of a friend is to support and confront," said Matt. "Not to fix, not to bail out of jail, not to lend money to. It's not for me to come riding in on a white horse like a knight in shining armor."

"I was planting nasturtiums when my daughter Dorothy drove up in her new car," Reggie said. "I knew something was wrong when I saw the mirror dangling on a wire and a big scratch on the door. Dorothy was crying when she got out of the car. I dropped my shovel and ran to her. Don't worry, I said, I can fix it. Let me get my tools. I ran into the garage and grabbed a few things and set about putting the mirror back together. But Dorothy just cried all the more.

"Somewhere along the line, I picked up the idea that I'm supposed to fix things. No matter what the problem, Daddy can fix it. But my daughter could have cared less about the car. She didn't need socket wrenches or hex nuts, she needed a hug. The thought of scratched paint was not even on the back porches of her mind. She said, 'Daddy, just hug me and tell me everything's alright.'"

"The lesson here is clear," said Matt. "Just because I'm an adult doesn't mean I need to fix things all the time, especially other people. Clocks, bicycles, and minor plumbing problems are okay. But I can't fix another human being. Reggie's daughter needed support and wanted to hear the same words I want to hear from my father: Don't worry. No matter what happens, everything will be alright."

Spiritual wisdom is where you find it

Tonight's meeting was an unusual one, tucked into the back of a store that sold Native American goods. The small room smelled of burning sage and was filled with the soft sound of a flute. This was my first "spiritual" meeting, based they said, on the spiritual aspects of AA. The topic was finding the spiritual path. The moderator, Red Thunder, spoke.

"I've heard it said that spirituality is a path toward a higher state of awareness. My brothers and I have used marijuana and peyote for years to attain this state."

"We just used 'em to get high," said a voice from the back.

"Hopefully the spiritual path will lead me toward perfection," said someone near the front.

"So, one hears," said the same joker in the back.

Red Thunder spoke again, "Today, I can reach out and be filled by the presence of The Great Spirit."

On the way back to the apartments I was lost in thought. It seemed to me that while religion might take me to spirituality, my journey to spirituality was not dependent on any religion. Rather, it was up to me to find my own path, one that worked for me.

The next day, Mike and I were talking in the hallway between sessions at the rehab center. Suddenly a middle-aged man, bearded, with longish hair, and dressed only in a bedsheet wrapped around him like a toga, emerged from a back room and wandered down the hall, dodging people as he went. His eyes were wild, his voice like that of a prophet. He bellowed out his message.

"The end is near, prepare to meet thy maker."

Mike and I looked at each other and laughed.

"Who are we?" yelled the prophet, "Why are we here?"

I asked Mike, "Is this the new spiritual counselor I heard about?"

"No," said Mike. "That's Crazy Larry. He's a pharmacist from New Bedford. Has a wife and six children and they run an organic farm."

"Oh," I said. "For a moment I thought he was going to lecture on metaphysics for the alcoholic."

"The meaning of life," shouted Crazy Larry. "What's the meaning of it all?" He waved his arms around like a madman.

"I think his roommates must have slipped LSD into his coffee again," said Mike, grinning.

Lindsey was a tall, sandy-haired pathologist from Knoxville who relapsed following the death of his youngest son, so this was his second trip through rehab. Despite his relapse, I sensed in him the recovery I wanted for myself, so I listened to what he had to say. After lunch one afternoon, we drove to a local mental health center to share a meeting. Timmy came with us.

During the ride, Lindsey shared some of his ideas with me. "I began my journey," he said, "with the spiritual principles described in the Big Book of AA. Some people say the program has a spiritual side. Others say it's more than that, it *is* a spiritual program."

We pulled onto the expressway. "But I yearned for more, so I decided to look for spiritual wisdom in the ancient scriptures from around the world. I began with the Hindu Bhagavad Gita. I had studied the Gita in college, but I remembered almost none of it. I was stunned when I picked up a copy, opened it to a random page and read, 'the spiritual path is one of attraction rather than promotion.'"

"Wow," I said, "that's the eleventh tradition of Alcoholics Anonymous almost word for word."

"Right. This truth was as valid when the Gita was written over 2,500 years ago, as it was in 1939 when the Big Book was written. There are also striking similarities between the Gita and the New Testament. I found the same principles in both books."

"Makes sense," I said, trying not to pontificate.

"So, I took what I could from the Gita and moved on to Buddhism. The Buddhists get a lot of good press in recovery circles and I wanted to know why."

After half an hour on the heralded Atlanta freeway, we had arrived at the mental health center and went inside. We continued our conversation on the way back to the apartments.

"Much of The Buddha's teaching struck a chord in me," said Lindsey. "I agreed with the idea that attachment to the temporary, material things of life only leads to suffering. When I was lost in my addiction, my worldly goods were of no help. I was intrigued with the thought that holding to lasting spiritual principles would bring serenity, joy, and peace."

"Happy, joyous, and free," I quoted the Big Book.

"To reach this place would require a lot of personal growth. I would have to change my way of thinking and my way of looking at the world. I started down that road with a lot of enthusiasm, and I know it's helped with my recovery."

"Like, how?" I asked.

"Well, if I can control my thinking, I can change my personality, change the worthless person I had become. My actions no longer have to be reflexive. I would no longer need the approval of others, and I could give up trying to be right," he said.

Umm, I thought, I liked the sound of this.

"Respect for life in all its forms is essential. Kindness and compassion are more useful than greed and anger."

"Tell me more," I said. I was eager to listen, something new for me.

"I had to deal with the idea that life was ephemeral, that nothing lasts. But then I realized that meant that life was constantly recreating itself, and each new moment was an opportunity for creativity and growth. You see, I think of life as something joyous and wonderful, a precious gift to be celebrated."

If only, I said to myself.

"Then I discovered something that surprised me." He grinned his sandy-haired smile at me. "I'm just as much a Christian as a Buddhist."

"Whoa!" I said. "Hold on there. You're saying that Jesus was a recovery dude? That doesn't square with the hellfire and brimstone my Christian brothers tried to shove down my throat."

"No, of course not," he said. "But if I looked at the words Jesus actually said, I saw that he was a revolutionary, always turning the world upside down."

"You mean, like, refusing to stone the woman caught in adultery?" I asked. "Or refusing to condemn the woman with five husbands? Or saying the meek would inherit the earth? Stuff like that?"

"Exactly. No more is it an eye for an eye, but now it's turn the other cheek," he said. "If the words attributed to him turned the world upside down then they probably were his words. If not, some zealous clerk may have added them later because he thought Jesus *should* have said them."

"Second, Jesus talked about states of mind, about how to think, and this radically changes how I interpret his sayings. For example, "Resist not evil," really makes no sense in the modern world. I doubt if he meant that we should have let Hitler overrun the world. But evil is also the negative thinking that lives inside my head. If I resist those thoughts with all my mental might, I give them power."

"So struggling against thoughts of using doesn't help," I said.

"It never did. Never helped me stop drinking," Lindsay said. "Only when I quit fighting my negative thoughts that they lose power over me."

"At some point, we quit fighting anything and everything," I quoted the Big Book again.

"But the most exciting idea is that the outer world is directed by the thoughts inside my head. Whatever I focus my attention on, it will be drawn to me. Not only that, but my thoughts actually shape the future, whether the thought is conscious or unconscious. As we hold these thoughts, and especially if we project them in prayer, they take form in front of me."

"Every thought in my head is a prayer," the words came out of my mouth, but I didn't say them. "If I think about cocaine all day, pretty soon I'll have it in my hand." I said that.

"But if I dump my negative thoughts and live in a world of positives, I'll draw good things to me," said Lindsay.

Later, I spoke with Mike and Robert about what Lindsey had said. They were skeptical.

"In other words," I paraphrased, "the spiritual treasure I keep in my heart will eventually become real in the world around me. If I harbor thoughts of revenge and resentment, of deception and meanness, then these qualities will become manifest in my world. If, on the other hand, I fill my heart with thoughts of improving myself and of making the world a better place, then my world will reflect the beauty and love in my heart. It's as simple as garbage in, garbage out."

Mike, a good Jewish boy, picked up Timmy's Bible, flipped to the Book of Matthew and began to read. "According to your faith, be it unto you."

"That does kind of shed a new light on things," said Robert, who, like me, had given up on Christian dogma. "I'm gonna have to think on this."

"I see what Leon meant," said Mike, "about trying to turn us sons of Abraham into good Christian boys. I've got some heavy thinking to do.'"

That evening I was alone in the apartment. All my roommates had gone home for the weekend, so I had the place to myself. All night I prayed, meditated, and thought about Lindsey's words. Lindsey came over the next morning, a Saturday, and we continued the most important conversation of my life.

"The real goal of all my striving is to find serenity," he said. "All the steps, the making of amends, exposing my worst secrets, all these are nothing but road signs on my way to developing a relationship with God. And the benefit of that relationship is nothing but heaven on earth."

The peace that passeth understanding.

"Heaven is real," he said, "and it exists here and now in this life in front of me and is accessible by me or anyone who seeks it."

The kingdom of God is at hand.

"I must avoid negativity in all its forms—bigotry, hatred, arrogance, spiritual pride, and the like."

If thine eye be evil, thy whole body shall be full of darkness.

"I must forgive all those who have wronged me. I must not judge others."

Forgive us our debts, as we forgive our debtors. Judge not, that ye be not judged.

"That since we are children of God, I should love all my fellows without limit, for we are all brothers."

This is my commandment, that ye love one another, as I have loved you.

"That a new man will be born, rising like a phoenix from the ashes of his old life."

Verily, verily, I say unto thee, except a man be born again, he cannot see the kingdom of God.

"And you will know the truth, and the truth shall set you free."

Dumbfounded, I had not spoken a word. Lindsey left the room silently and I was alone again. I laid my head on the couch pillow and slept. When I awoke, the soft afternoon light was flooding through the window. I knew what I needed to do. Finally, it all made sense.

I stayed up all night, drinking hot tea, praying, and thinking.

A lesson and the blessing

It was late afternoon and the sky was overcast as Timmy and I walked back to the apartment.

"I heard that your discharge was denied," said Timmy. "Weren't you supposed to leave next week? What happened?"

"Right after lunch, Matt called me into his office. I have some bad news, he said. Staff canceled your discharge. I was heartbroken. I've been here over six months and my heart was set on going home for Thanksgiving. I broke out in tears, started to get angry, then I remembered what Father Mick said."

"You mean 'In everything, there's a lesson and a blessing?' asked Timmy. "That no matter what happens, whether it seems a joy or a sorrow, it can help me?"

"I didn't expect to put the idea into practice quite so soon," I said. "I tried to overcome my emotions and find the lesson. Maybe, high expectations, low serenity. Or that I shouldn't count my chickens before they hatch. Or that I wasn't the best judge of my own mental state. And the blessing? Maybe by staying an extra month I could avoid the relapses I've been seeing all around me. Immediately I felt better. Not happy, but better."

"I'm sorry," grinned Timmy, "but look on the bright side, you'll have my wonderful company for another month."

Life is not as hard as it seems

We were doing the weekly grocery shopping at Food World. Robert was checking out the dessert section.

"You okay, my friend?" Mike asked, putting eggs into our cart. "You've got a strange look on your face."

"I've been thinking about something.," I sighed.

"I told you not to do that," he said.

"I can't help it." I grinned. "It's in my nature. If I must give up my old ideas, if everything I think I know is wrong, then I have a problem."

"Do tell."

"It always seemed that life was hard," I said. "It beat me over the head at every turn. But if everything I think I know is wrong, then life isn't hard. Life is easy. Eh?"

"The Big Book says that our lives should be happy, joyous, and free from fear."

Robert joined us. In the checkout line we overheard two women talking ahead of us.

"You know, Susie," whispered the first, "Sex gives me a real pain in the ass." Her friend Susie thought for a second, then grinned devilishly.

"If sex is giving you a pain in the ass," she said, "honey, you doin' it wrong."

We snickered to ourselves.

Later at lunch, we continued our conversation.

"You know," said Mike, "that lady might just as well have said, 'If life is giving you a pain in the ass, you're doing it wrong.' Let me give you an example."

I nodded.

"When I was an undergraduate," he said, "the hardest course I ever took was College Physics."

I had taken the same course and it was rough. "Yeah," I said, "an airplane leaves Detroit at 2:30 pm flying 37 degrees northwest against a crosswind of 67 degrees at 45 miles an hour. When do they get to Miami?"

"Something like that. One day I realized I'd spent four hours on one problem and was beating my head against the wall. Finally, I went outside with a cup of coffee and a cigarette and considered my situation. Then I was struck with a moment of clarity."

"By a what?" I laughed.

"A moment of clarity, you yo-yo! I suddenly understood something that had baffled me."

"Okay," I continued to laugh, "What was this great epiphany?"

"That I was making the problems too hard. The homework I'd been given was simply not that difficult. If it was taking me four hours to work one problem, obviously I was doing it wrong."

"It wasn't because you were lousy in physics, was it?"

"No. Now shut up and listen. It was because I was making the problems harder than they were supposed to be. I went back inside and worked all twenty problems in just under two hours. Voila! If life seems difficult, maybe I'm doing it wrong."

"What a great idea," I said. "You should write a book."

"No, my friend, you're the writer, not me. You'll write the book."

"And you'll kibitz?"

"Of course!"

I'm Starting to Wake Up

I am responsible for the consequences of
my actions.

My using can no longer blind me to my
mistakes and misdeeds.

I can't change the world, only how I respond to it.

With my newfound way of looking at the world,
I found spiritual wisdom all around me.

Deep spiritual wisdom has been with mankind
since the shepherds gazed at the stars.

Each religion has the kernel of truth at
its core, no matter how badly men have twisted it.

In everything, there is a lesson and a blessing,
but I have to remember to look for it.

We realized that we no longer had to fight
anything or anybody, that the peace we sought
was always with us.

Life is easy, and if it seems otherwise, maybe
you're doing it wrong.

Living by Spiritual Principles

"The goal of life
is to make your heartbeat match the beat of the universe,
to match your nature with Nature."
—Joseph Campbell

Carry the message

"In AA, we are told that our job is to carry the message to the alcoholic who still suffers," said Dr. Taylor. This was a mandated lecture, and all the drunks and junkies at the center were assembled in the auditorium. "So, what exactly *is* the message?" We waited expectantly for the wisdom of the physician who had founded the center. He picked up the Big Book of AA and began to read.

Living by Spiritual Principles

"Quite as important was the discovery that spiritual principles would solve all my problems," he read, then looked out across his audience. "The message then is simple—that living by spiritual principles will solve my problems—all my problems—including my addiction. It doesn't matter what you understand your Higher Power to be, only that you have one you can believe in. That, and you must be willing to live by these spiritual precepts."

He held the Big Book up. "In this book, you'll find the stories of the founders of our fellowship, and of how they used these ideas to overcome their disease. They found that relying on such values was not optional but that their new life required strict adherence to them, and that failure to do so resulted in a quick return to addiction."

He put the book down and stared out at us. His gaze seemed almost pleading.

"Unless each of you completes the work required by the Steps and reaches recovery, your death at the hands of your disease is certain. our return to the pit of addiction will be directly related to your failure to follow these principles in your everyday life. These ideas are not pie-in-the-sky platitudes to be recited at an AA meeting; they must be our constant guide, in our thoughts, our words, and our actions."

"This new way of life not only frees us from the hell of our illness, but from the fear, worry, and hurt feelings of life itself. Acceptance brings serenity and a life filled with peace and happiness. The benefits of these blessings far outweigh a life driven by self-will."

"What, pray tell, are these wonderful and mysterious principles?" he asked. "In our hearts, we already know them, but our egos have buried them deep in the darkness of our denial. I charge you now with opening your hearts and rediscovering the moral values required for our new lives. Good day and good luck to you all."

Judge not

We were sitting in the lounge trying to avoid judging the decaf coffee. Raphael sat with us. "The only way I could stay sober was to quit judging other people," he said.

"Judging others puts limitations on them, and by association, on me," Leon said, beaming.

"Living without limitations," I said. "I don't understand."

"I'm sure you tried living without restrictions," said Raphael. "No limit to the amount of drugs or alcohol you could consume, but that's not what I'm talking about. See Mountain Jack over there?"

I grinned. Mountain Jack had come in last night from somewhere in the backwoods of Tennessee. Long-haired and woodsy, he made a stark contrast to the professional-looking people around him.

"If I told you he had an IQ of 85, pumped gas, and cooked meth in his basement, would you accept that?" asked Raphael. I looked at Mountain Jack and nodded.

"But what if I told you he had an IQ of 185 and was a tenured if somewhat eccentric professor of mathematics and physics at the state university?"

"I'd say I had badly misjudged him," I said. "Judging him by his outward appearances, I limited what I thought of him."

"When you limit what you think of others, you necessarily limit not only them but yourself," said Raphael, echoing Leon's words.

"But it's almost impossible not to judge," I said. "For example, every time I see a person jogging, I want to put them down, because I can't make it around the track even once. They're doing a lot better than my fat tubby self, but I'd never admit it. I guess I'm afraid they're better than me."

"By judging this world and the people in it, I'm in essence judging God's handiwork. Not something I do well," said Leon.

"It also makes you arrogant," said Raphael.

"Not me," said Timmy, grinning.

More useful

Robert came bouncing into the living room, plopped down on the couch, and kicked off his flip-flops.

"I've just had a great idea. Everyone sit down and listen to this," he said.

"No controlling behavior here," said Mike.

"Hush," said Robert, "I have the floor."

"And most of the couch, too," I laughed.

"Okay, here it is," said Robert. "You know how Matt said we shouldn't judge. Yet every time we use the words good and bad, we're making a value judgment. We're saying that, for example, the rain is good, if my garden needs it, but bad, if I can't play golf."

"Yeah," said Timmy, "who gave Robert the right to judge the rain, anyway?"

"Timmy," said Robert, "sometimes I wonder about you, and then sometimes I just wonder."

"I see what you're saying," I said. "I mean, is the rain is not inherently good or bad. It's just water falling from the sky."

"Yeah," said Mike. "I remember being taught that World War II was a good war and that Vietnam was a bad war. I guess a war could be useful, but I can't imagine the idea that any war is ever good."

"But how can any of us go through the day without using those words?" asked Leon. "Good and bad are so ingrained in my everyday vocabulary, I'm not sure I can do without them."

"Here's what I propose," said Robert: "that we use the terms more useful and less useful. More useful suggests we're moving toward a goal, while less useful suggests we're moving away from that goal."

"And we wouldn't have to judge anything," said Timmy.

The Golden Rule

We invited Father Mick to join us for lunch at the cafeteria. Robert, Timmy, Mike, and I chipped in to buy his meal. We were wrestling with the concept of loving your neighbor—in the real world. We wanted to hear his take on the Golden Rule.

"Every religion, culture, or ethical tradition I know of," said Father Mick, "has some variation on the Golden Rule. Christians claim the saying for themselves, but they can be a tad self-righteous at times." He grinned.

"But if I actually follow the Golden Rule," asked Timmy, "won't other people just run over the top of me?"

"Only if you let them," said Father Mick. "Nothing in recovery says you have to lie down and let people walk all over on you."

"Does that mean that whatever goes around comes around?" asked Robert, scraping the last of the chocolate pudding from his bowl.

"Certainly, we reap what we sow," said Father Mick. "But you should've learned by now that you're responsible for the effects of the decisions you make. If I plant hatred and resentments, I will harvest the same. If I plant love and kindness, they will be my harvest .If I want to be treated with respect, I must first treat others with respect. If I want to be treated honestly, I must treat others the same way."

Mike spoke, "If I'm kind to others, they're more likely to be kind to me. If I'm rude to someone on the phone, well, you get it."

"Sugar draws more flies than vinegar," said Robert, surveying the chocolate on his fingers. "That's definitely true."

"If someone's mean to me," asked Timmy, "shouldn't I be mean back to them?"

"No my son," said Father Mick. "My kindness may not be returned, but I will be made better by the act. And the person you're in conflict with will eventually benefit as well. Planting the seeds of love is never wrong."

"No matter what the question," said Timmy, "the answer is love."

Robert finished licking his fingers and said, "To quote The Buddha, never impose on others what you would not choose for yourself."

We were back in the apartments, flopped on the couch and the floor. We were discussing the idea of kindness.

Robert raised his hand. "My turn," he said. "Me next."

After much moaning and groaning by the audience, Robert was allowed to share.

"I was at the back of a long, slow-moving checkout line at the superstore. The people ahead of me were fuming at the delay. The young cashier seemed incapable of finding the right price or correctly running her register, the only open one in the store. Her supervisor, standing behind her, was not happy."

"After what seemed like an eternity of waiting, I reached the front of the line. I could see the hurt in the cashier's eyes and I could feel her pain."

"Having a rough day? I asked her.

"She spoke softly as she rang up my items. 'You don't know the half of it,' she said. She looked up at the clock on the wall. It was 5:45 pm. he said, 'I was supposed to pick up my kids at 5. They're waiting for me at the daycare center. Their teachers get really mad when I'm late and take it out on my kids.'"

"The tears began to well up in her eyes and her nose was running."

"She said, I've had this stupid cold for over a week and I just can't shake it. And I've had to pee for over an hour, but I can't get away from this frigging register."

"'Don't worry,' I said. Everything's gonna be alright.'"

"She looked at me like a long-lost friend. 'You really think so?'"

"'Of course,' I answered. 'Things always work themselves out if I just let them.' I handed her a tissue and she wiped her face and blew her nose.

"'I guess you're right,' she said. "I'm lucky to have this job. My husband's been out of work for over two months."

"I said, don't be afraid, you're not alone."

"'I know,'" she said, "but sometimes I forget.' She smiled and it lit up her face.

"After she checked me out, her smile lingered. Those in the line began to smile as well. In a few moments, her relief arrived, and she headed for the bathroom and then was on her way to pick up her children."

Great big yellow buttery balls of love

The next morning the air was warm and the sun felt good on my bare arms as we sat on the patio behind the rehab center.

Timmy spoke, "Look, guys, love may be the answer, but it's hard to remember that when a five-hundred-pound gorilla is sitting on my chest. Most days I don't have to fight gorillas, it just seems that way. The idea that love is the answer seems so far-fetched it can't possibly be true, can it?"

"Maybe," said Mike, lighting a cigarette. "How could love possibly be the answer to anything in the real world? Well, what is the gorilla sitting on my desk? Mostly it's my relationships with other people, like my boss who won't give me a raise, my kids who want $100 tennis shoes, and the banker who won't lend me any money. It's ordinary people with aching feet who were up all night with a crying baby. And let's not forget the problems that fly around inside my head. Old ways of thinking, resentments, fears. These are my gorillas."

"To make a change," said Reggie, "first I have to recognize that my problem is me."

Timmy nodded. "My name is Timmy and my problem is Timmy."

"I need to find a new way of thinking," Mike said, blowing smoke into the air, "to get me out of the gorilla cage. And I'm not just blowing smoke here." Mike laughed but coughed when he did.

Reggie said, "Try this. I call it Great Big Yellow Buttery Balls of Love. I use it when I have to see my mother-in-law, ask the boss for a raise, or know I'm gonna butt heads with someone."

" It may sound a little like science fiction, but...." He gave us his best imitation of Rod Serling: "Imagine, if you will"—Robert started making Twilight Zone music with his nose—"Imagine, if you will, a yellow ball, the size of a beach ball, covered with gobs of yellow gooey buttery love. Dripping yellow sunny buttery balls of love. Hold it over your head and throw it. Like this." He heaved his imaginary big yellow buttery ball of love toward the horizon.

"Now," said Reggie, "this is the best part, you don't have to know where to aim it. It's like a cruise missile, just tell it where to go and it will. For example, you might want to throw one at your pissed wife. Go on, try it!"

Timmy looked sheepish but did as instructed, reaching back over his head and throwing an imaginary great big yellow buttery ball of love in the general direction of his wife. He grinned.

"It seems silly ..." he said.

"Sure it does," said Reggie. "It makes you smile just to do it. But I swear, it works every time."

Later, Reggie told me the idea of great big yellow buttery balls of love was just another way of asking God's blessing for the person I'm in conflict with.

"It works both ways," he said. "The blessing always comes back to me."

Integrity

Tomorrow was skit day. Each residence group was required to perform a three-minute skit on some topic of recovery. The reward was a free pizza dinner for the winners. We were, quite predictably, having trouble getting organized.

"Everybody shut up and let's get on with this thing," said John, the most anal-retentive of us all. "We have to present a three-minute skit at 10 am. in the morning, and it's almost midnight. I for one would like to finish and go to bed."

"I thought we were doing Hamlet?" said Timmy.

"No problem," said Robert, tongue in cheek. "We should be able to boil down a three-hour play to three minutes without much problem."

Reggie reached in his pocket and pulled out his three-month AA chip.

"Here it is," he said. "Read what's on the back of the chip, 'To thine own self be true.'"

"Yeah," said Mike. "We ought to be able to talk about integrity for three minutes."

"Does that mean I don't get to wear tights?" asked Timmy.

"No tights and no sword fights," said Mike. "Let's stay on point here. Can anybody define integrity?"

The room fell silent.

"We're a bunch of drunks and junkies," said Robert. "What the hell do we know about integrity?"

"Maybe more than you think," said Timmy. "Like Reggie said, it's on the back of all the AA chips. It must have something to do with recovery, I guess."

"If I'm true to myself, I'm no longer dependent on the opinions of others," said Reggie. "It's a freeing feeling."

"And frightening," said Timmy.

"If I'm a child of God and I'm true to myself, doesn't that mean I'm true to that piece of God that shines within me?" asked Robert.

"Well put, kind sir," said Reggie. "Of course, it means I'm true to my relationship with God. I don't have a significant relationship with my liver or my Jack Daniels. At least not anymore."

"Can I be Polonius?" asked Timmy.

"If I'm true to myself," said Robert, "I'll necessarily be true to my fellows. Emmet Fox said it like this, cost what it will, involve what it may, the integrity of the soul must be preserved."

So, we had our topic.

Golden throated Leon narrated, "And now, let's give it up for these guys, your very own Foreskins of the Apocalypse, presenting a somewhat abbreviated version of Hamlet by the immortal bard, William Shakespeare! Let's give it up for the boys in tights!"

Timmy bounded onto the stage in black tights and a short white wig, brandishing a Star Wars light saber and singing To Thine Own Self Be True, to a chorus of catcalls and kazoos. The musical Hamlet, in three minutes or less, was a roaring success. We enjoyed the pizza.

Acceptance

A thin gray rain filled the sky outside. Inside, the apartment seemed especially cozy and warm. I yawned, then quickly covered my mouth. It Sunday morning and the aroma of coffee and bacon was delicious in the air.

"I have a lot of trouble accepting a world that's full of evil," said Timmy. "How can a loving God allow wars, misery, and poverty on such a grand scale?"

Wee Willy had smelled the bacon too, and invited himself for breakfast said. Grinning, he said, "It all comes down to acceptance and how I see the world," he said. "To find happiness, I must change the way I see the world."

Robert picked up the Big Book of AA and began to read:

"... acceptance is the answer to all my problems today. When I am disturbed, it is because some person, place, thing or situation—some fact of my life—is unacceptable to me, and I can find no serenity until I accept that person, place, thing or situation as being exactly the way it is supposed to be at this moment...Until I could accept my alcoholism, I could not stay sober; unless I accept life completely on life's terms, I cannot be happy. I need to concentrate not so much on what needs to be changed in the world, as on what needs to be changed in me and my attitudes."

"So, what's the answer to Timmy's problem with the world?" asked Robert.

"First, the definition of evil is important," said Mike. "The best one I've found is simply, man's inhumanity to man. God doesn't rain evil down upon the world, we generate it for ourselves."

"We're the ones who brought slavery, bigotry, genocide, and all the other tribulations into the world," said Robert. "God gave us free will to make decisions for ourselves. You can't blame him when our decisions end up hurting others."

"But I don't want to live in a world with Adolf Hitler and the Ku Klux Klan," said Timmy. "I try to accept that these things exist, but it still upsets me to no end."

"It's not your world, Timmy," said Wee Willy, sincere like never before. "It's God's world. Who are you to judge God's handiwork? Who died and made you king?"

"In other words," said Robert, "If God is perfect, as many of us believe, then his world must be perfect, too. Life is perfect just the way it is."

"I don't know," said Timmy, shaking his head.

"I'm the one who puts the spin on things," said Wee Willy. "As the Bard said, there is no thing good or bad, except my thinking makes it so."

"I always thought that perfection was getting everything, well, perfect," I said. "If I took a test with a hundred questions and got a hundred right, that was perfect. If I got ninety-nine right, it was a good score, but it wasn't perfect."

"I'll bet that got you into trouble," said John.

"Yeah," I said, "I expected a perfection that was beyond my reach. So I was chronically disappointed."

"Think of it this way," said Mike. 'They say God created all women beautiful, if only I have the eyes to see it. In the same way, the world is perfect, if only I have the eyes to see it. To overcome my old way of living, they say, I must acquire new eyes. Cast out the old eyes that saw ugliness and evil everywhere in exchange for eyes that can see beauty and truth all around me.

"But acceptance isn't enough," said Robert, peering over John's shoulder to check on the status of breakfast. "I must embrace life as it is. Acceptance with understanding and love will lead me to serenity."

"God let me accept the world as it is, without the need to judge it," said Wee Willy.

There's no way, I thought, no way I'm ever gonna be able to do this.

Sanity

We were walking back to the van following the Starlight meeting. Something about a spiritual meeting under a canopy of stars brought out our most philosophical thoughts.

"When I first got here, Matt told me that everything I thought I knew was wrong," I said. "Of course, I didn't believe him. Matt told me nothing would do, but that I had to dump all the garbage in my head and start from scratch, replacing every bit of misinformation with a new way of thinking."

"A totally new way of living," said Mike.

"I thought he was trying to brainwash me," I said.

"Your brain needed a good washing," said Robert, laughing.

"The idea of replacing everything, every old idea about living, of redefining my place in the universe, was overwhelming," said Mike. "Fortunately, Matt said I didn't have to do it all at once. I could take baby steps."

"Baby steps," said Timmy, giggling.

"How's that going for you?" asked Robert.

"Better," said Mike.

Leon took advantage of the lull in the conversation to begin one of his tirades.

"Sanity," he said, "comes from the Latin, *sanitas*, meaning soundness of mind or right reason. Wholeness. Health."

I nodded and was grateful that my coffee cup was full.

"Wholeness, of course, is the object of healing and health," he said. "Usually a sign of your sanity."

"Sanity, wholeness, health. I got that. Go on," said Robert.

"But more importantly, wholeness is the essence of holiness! This includes peace of mind, prosperity, even spiritual harmony. So, whole, holy, healing, and sanity are all related."

"What's the punch line?" I quipped.

Leon grinned. "To find my sanity means to be made whole again. To be made whole is to regain my health, in mind, body, and spirit. New thinking that puts me on the spiritual path will return me to sanity by reconnecting me to the source my holiness."

New thinking? A new way of living? The thought roiled through my mind. Was that really possible?

LIVING BY SPIRITUAL PRINCIPLES

The result of all my efforts is a total change in my character: A total and complete psychic rearrangement has occurred.

I have found a new set of priorities to guide my behavior.

An essential part of our new life is to re-establish the old relationships we lost in the days of our using.

If I want to find forgiveness for my errors, I must first forgive all those I even think have wronged me.

I need to make amends for the wrongs I have done to others. Not just apologize, but never commit the same offense again.

The hardest part of recovery may be learning to think more of others than myself.

The goal of recovery is not just sobriety, but a life that is happy, joyous, and free of fear.

Serenity, also known as enlightenment, nirvana, and heaven on earth, comes unbidden when I pursue the spiritual pathway.

Happiness cannot be found in the outside world. But it follows serenity as a puppy dog.

A New Way of Living

> *"Beauty is truth, truth beauty,—that is all*
> *Ye know on earth, and all ye need to know."*
> —John Keats

Seeing with new eyes

We were walking in the mall, sipping our Orange Juliuses, and heading for the movie theatre. We walked slowly to maximize the staring time at the female children of God as they passed. We tried our best to enforce the ten second rule: If you stare at a woman for more than ten seconds, you're no longer admiring the handiwork of God, but have moved over to lust, which was to be discouraged.

"Keats said, Beauty is Truth, Truth Beauty," Robert said. "The beauty of a woman is not in her external appearance, but in the Godhead that shines from within. If I can see that, I can see the real Beauty of her person. And seeing that Beauty, that perfection, I see the Truth of her divinity. Our divinity. Beauty is Truth."

We sauntered slowly past several good examples of Beauty and Truth before Reggie spoke.

"Now take the next step," said the preacher, "the world is beautiful just as it is, if only I have the eyes to see it."

That's all ye know on earth, and all ye need to know, I thought to myself.

"He that hath eyes to hear, let him see," said Reggie under his breath.

Change in character

Matt was a few minutes late to his morning group session. He took off his raincoat and shook the rain from it, for the day had begun with a steady downpour. He smiled, hung up his coat and asked, "How do I go about changing my character for the better." When no one answered, he began.

"The problem," Matt said, "is that habits of thinking are tenacious. Tough to overcome. Especially if we're only halfhearted about giving them up. New ideas may live in our minds, but until they make their way into the subconscious—the heart, if you will—and are incorporated into the whole person, a change of character isn't possible."

"'As a man thinketh in his own heart, so is he,'" quoted Leon. "Proverbs, I believe."

"A change in character," said Matt, "which is what we're seeking, is a change in the soul. Such a change produces a new and different person. It's only in the heart where these changes can occur."

"'Keep thy heart with all diligence, for out of it are the issues of life,'" said Leon. "Proverbs again."

"Once a real change in character happens," said Matt, "the new man, the new Adam, will forever think and act differently. Such a change may come about slowly, as he works his way through recovery, but it will happen. He'll experience a new way of reacting to the world. His old motivating force, fear, will be replaced by love."

"But…how can I do this?" asked Timmy.

"Anyone?" said Matt, looking around the room. "Who can answer Timmy's question?"

"Prayer," said Mike and Robert together. "Prayer."

"Yes, of course," said Matt.

Establish new priorities

As I entered the cafeteria, I saw Mike sitting near the window. He had a newcomer with him and was hitting him both barrels. Mike must have been running short on ammunition, for he waved at me to join them.

"There are a lot of ways to look at the program of recovery," said Mike, looking over at me. "Right?"

I nodded as I bit into my sandwich.

Mike waited until I swallowed. "My roommate here likes to talk about the value of reordering priorities," he said.

Trapped by my friend, I sized up our new companion. Wendell was a dentist from Alabama. He had a pencil-thin mustache and looked like he just stepped out of a 1950s cigarette commercial. He stared at us with the eyes of a deer caught in the headlights.

"Hello," I said, reaching across the table to shake his hand. His palm was wet. "Relax. No one's going to bite you. When did you get in?"

"Early this morning," he squeaked.

"What brought you here?" I asked.

"They told me if I didn't come, they'd take away my dental license. They caught me snorting nitrous oxide." He hung his head. "After work on Friday, I rolled a tank of the laughing gas into my office and sat in my chair with the prongs in my nose. I planned on spending just an hour or so getting high before going home. But on Monday morning my staff found me unconscious in my chair, still hooked up to the nitrous."

"Sounds bad. What're you going to do?" I asked.

"I have no idea," said the dentist. "I guess that's why I'm here. I don't know how any of this happened to me."

"Maybe your priorities are screwed up," said Mike. He kicked me under the table.

"Okay, okay. Wendell—it is Wendell, isn't it?" The new fish nodded weakly. "There are lots of ways to look at recovery, but my favorite is as a reordering of priorities. Got that?"

Wendell nodded again.

"What's the most important thing in your life?" I asked.

"Now, you mean?" asked Wendell. "Uh, Molly would have to be first, I guess."

"Is Molly your daughter or your wife?" I asked.

Wendell laughed and his face flushed. "Well, actually, she's my mistress."

"That'll have to change," said Mike. "You can't have an affair and be in recovery."

"The most important thing in my life has to be my sobriety," I said. "Getting sober and nothing else."

"I don't think I follow you there," said Wendell.

"That's okay," interrupted Mike. "I didn't think you would."

"My first priority is my relationship with God," I said. "My sobriety is my recovery is my relationship with God. Only a Higher Power will protect me from relapsing."

"But there's more," I said. "And this is critically important. Anything I place above my sobriety, I'll lose."

"That's why I can't get sober for my wife, my kids, or my job," said Mike. If my mistress is more important to me, I'll make decisions for her over my sobriety. My focus won't be my recovery. I'll eventually drink again, and I'll lose both my sobriety and my mistress."

"My second priority has to be my family," I said. "Other than my Higher Power, they're the most reliable source of support and love I'll ever have."

"And the new number three?" asked Wendell.

"Learning to think more about others than myself," Mike said.

Go toward your goal

"There are a lot of manic-depressives in this room," said Matt.

A rumble approaching a roar spread through the classroom.

"One of our character traits is the inability to stay on track, to stay focused, even if you're not bipolar," he said. "We're easily distracted. We've been accused of never finishing anything."

"Enlighten us, O great master," said Mike.

"Okay, I will," said Matt. "Go toward your goal. In life I need to ask myself, will my decision take me toward my goal or away from my goal? When confronted with a fork in the road ahead, take the path that leads you toward your goal."

"Should I study for my test tomorrow," said Timmy, "or should I go the pharmacy and shoot up Ritalin? Makes sense to me. Let's go to the pharmacy."

"You have a broken thinker," said Matt, smiling.

"Still toxic," shouted Mike from the back of the room.

"But you get the idea," said Matt. "It's your own personal Occam's razor."

"What the hell is that?" Timmy whispered to me.

"Never mind," I said. "Just do what he says."

Forming new habits

"The psychologist William James said it takes three weeks to form new habits," said Raleigh, tonight's speaker. "For me, it took a lot longer. I had to keep on keeping on when I really didn't want to. Repeatedly, I felt too tired to go to a meeting, too stuck in my self-pity to talk to anyone. The telephone weighed a hundred pounds."

"But I held on to the idea that if I persevered, I could make this whole recovery thing work. Then they showed me a bunch of new habits, ones that would affect my everyday life, just as my using had done. I have a list here," he said, fumbling in his shirt pocket.

He read, "First thing in the morning, say a little prayer. Something simple, like 'God I thank you for keeping me clean and sober today.' After a cup of coffee, settle down and read something spiritual, like the Daily Reflections. Then meditate on what you've read and how it applies to your life today. All this before you head out the door."

"In the evening, go to a meeting. Get the name and phone number of another alcoholic at each meeting. Make a point of arriving early and staying late." He looked up. "You know, the meeting before the meeting, and the meeting after the meeting."

"Call your sponsor every day. Read at least one page of the Big Book of AA before bedtime. Review how your day went, the problems you encountered, and the mistakes you made, and consider how you can do better the next day. And, of course, as you lay your head on the pillow, say a little prayer, sometimes nothing more than, thank you."

Making decisions

The Triangle AA meeting house was in the middle of the strip club region of Atlanta and was surrounded by bars on all sides. A good place for an AA meeting, Mike said. The best-attended meeting in the city, it was not uncommon to have fifty or more show up on a Saturday night. The chairperson asked the group for a discussion topic and Timmy raised his hand.

"What about doing the next right thing?" asked Timmy. The chairperson agreed and opened the floor for sharing.

"If I can remember to do it," said a lady near us.

"I ask myself, what are my motives?" said another woman. "Am I pursuing my own self-interests, or am I actually trying to do some good?"

"I get carried away by events and don't stop to think," said Vera, who rode with us to the meeting.

"You know what Fozzie the Bear said, don't ya?" whispered Robert. Not waiting for a response, he said, "When you come to a fork in the road, take it." I grinned and poked him in the ribs.

A young man in the front said, "Every day, I have a hundred decisions to make." He was dressed in mechanic's garb and his hands were stained with grease. "I try to imagine that God is sitting on my shoulder, watching and helping me. What would he want me to do? That's how I decide."

Another woman spoke. She couldn't have been more than sixteen. "I've been in the program for two years. At first, I had a lotta trouble with doing the next right thing, but I'm getting better at it. With practice, life gets easier."

"I ask myself, will this decision take me toward my goal or away from my goal?" said the chairperson. "Of course, it depends upon what my goal is. For me, the goal is recovery. Will this decision help or hinder my sobriety?"

On the way home, Vera said, "If our job is to bring God's love into the world, then all my decisions should be made out of that love."

"You're starting to sound like a Hallmark greeting card," said Mike.

"Life does have its risks," I said.

"Great big yellow buttery balls of love," said Robert as we pulled up to the apartments.

"Great big yellow...Hee, hee," said Timmy, snickering.

Material possessions

Mike came out of the apartment and the two of us headed down the path to rehab. He smiled.

"My daughter sent me this new T-shirt," he said. On the front of the shirt was a phrase written in Gaelic.

"What does it say?" I asked, pointing to the indecipherable writing.

"It's Celtic," he said. "Whoever dies with the most toys wins! Wanna play that game?"

"No thanks," I said. "I already did—and lost."

Wee Willy was leading the morning spiritual. We slipped quietly into the back of the room, late as usual.

"...if I sweated bullets to buy something, made layaway payments, waited months for it, I could become very attached to my material dream—a new car, a college education for my kid. I can clutch my possessions with unbelievable tightness, afraid I'll lose them. A path based on material goods will always be governed by fear. But I have a choice—love of money, or love of God. As I let go of the former, the latter will fill my heart and direct my actions."

Robert whispered in my ear, "No man can serve two masters: for either he will hate the one and love the other; or else he will hold to the one and despise the other. Ye cannot serve God and mammon."

"All material possessions will eventually fail me," said Wee Willy. "Light bulbs burn out, cars break down, the roof leaks. Nothing worldly lasts, so if I put my faith in worldly goods, I shouldn't be surprised if I am constantly being disappointed. Only the foolish man builds his house on the sand."

"Besides," Wee Willy continued, "as an alcoholic and addict, my problems were never solved by money. In fact, the more money I earned, the more I spent on booze, gambling, and women."

Robert whispered to me again, "My daughter once told me cocaine was God's way of telling me I was making too much money."

"Hey," said a voice from the back of the room, "does that mean I have to give up my new Jaguar?"

"No," said Wee Willy, "but it does mean I have to give up on the idea that material possessions are the measure of my success. My goals in life must change."

"So, I can keep my Jaguar?" said the voice.

"In your case," said Wee Willy, "go and sell all thy hast and give it to the poor, and thou shalt have treasure in heaven."

"Oh, shit," moaned the voice.

Quit playing games you can't win

Vera and I drove to Fulton County Detox to mingle with the residents and learn from their mistakes. The drunks and junkies there were rescued from the drunk tank or pulled out from under bushes. A few checked themselves in voluntarily. Three days was the usual stay before they were turned back out onto the street. Their care was paid for by the county.

They brought Leroy to detox instead of letting him spend the night in the drunk tank, a kindness of the policeman who picked him up. Leroy worked day labor and every day after work he walked to the local mini-market and bought a pack of cigarettes and a bottle of wine. Then he'd sit down on a street corner under a shade tree and drink his wine in the cool of the afternoon. About this time, the local police sector car would roll and arrest him for public drunkenness.

"I just don't understand," he said. "That officer keeps arresting me over and over. I don't know why he don't leave me alone. I just want to drink my wine."

"How many times has he picked you up for drinking in public?" I asked.

"Oh, I don't know. Maybe twenty or fifty times."

On the way back to the center, Vera put on a tape by Father Martin, a Catholic priest famous for his talks on alcoholism. Today's story was about an alcoholic who climbed into the ring with Mike Tyson every day, and every day came out bloody.

"This alcoholic comes out of his hotel room one morning and Mike Tyson is sparring in the ballroom, getting ready for a championship bout," said Father Martin. "The alcoholic thinks, you know I used to be on the boxing team in college. Sure, that was twenty years ago, but I bet I could take him. Our friend climbs in the ring, gets soundly trounced, then slinks out of the ring, saying, I'll never do that again."

"The next day our friend passes the ballroom again, thinking, I did a little shadowboxing yesterday afternoon and I bet I could take Mike on. He climbs in the ring and gets pasted. He crawls out, saying, 'I'll never do that again.'

"On the third day, our friend gets a sudden uncontrollable urge and without thinking jumps into the ring, with the same result as before. He gets his ass whipped. Again, he slithers out of the ring, saying, 'I'll never do that again.'

"Our pugilistic friend is like every alcoholic," said Father Martin. "He continually thinks that someday he will be able to drink alcohol like a normal person. But each time, alcohol whips his butt. Now, AA has a very simple solution to this problem."

He paused for emphasis.

"Don't get in the ring."

Hostages

I arrived late to Matt's group, dodged eye contact with him, and slunk into a seat at the very back of the room. Timmy was speaking.

"But I thought ..." said Timmy.

"I told you not to do that," said Robert, shaking his head. "Relationships are difficult for alcoholics. Somehow we never learned how to behave in the world."

"Yes," said Matt. "Either we're fear-driven and trying to hold onto someone with chains of iron, or we devote ourselves to another person so completely that we subjugate our personality to theirs. Both extremes are deadly."

"We don't have relationships," said Mike. "We take hostages. It's taken me months to realize how I did that to my ex-wife."

"Can one alcoholic marry another?" asked Vera. "What about dating a compulsive gambler?"

"A recovering addict cannot live with a using partner without relapsing," said Matt. "I've seen it repeatedly. Two recovering alcoholics can have a relationship, but the lack of emotional maturity usually dooms the effort. Not impossible, but difficult. And don't forget, no relationships until you've been sober for at least a year!"

"I was afraid you'd say that," said Vera.

"From somewhere," said Matt, "we came up with the idea that we own our partners. We never learned how to set healthy boundaries."

"What are boundaries?" asked Timmy. "All I know is that as I get closer to some people, my relationships get all sticky and mushy. I found I couldn't say no, which got me into endless trouble."

"That's not uncommon," said Matt. "Boundaries are necessary to maintain my individuality. I can't merge myself with another person."

"I always expected the other person to complete me and solve all my problems," said John. "I thought we had to be soul mates bound in perfect love nests, like mating octopi."

"It's no wonder you've been married three times," Matt said, grinning. "It's not healthy to be instantly intimate with a stranger, either conversationally or sexually. The second date between two AA members usually consists of backing up the U-Haul trailer. It just doesn't work."

Relationships

Father Mick joined our afternoon house meeting to talk about sex relations. We were all dying to hear what a Catholic priest could tell us about sex.

"All my relationships with women were built on physical attraction," Mike began. "The first time the two of us were alone together, we ended up in bed."

"Umm," I mumbled, unwilling to admit that the same had been true for me.

"Then I'd wake up one morning and ask myself, how the hell did I get myself in this mess?" he continued. "But by then it was too late to get out."

"What you're saying," said Father Mick, "is that perhaps you should get to know a woman before taking her to bed?"

"I'm afraid you're right," said Mike, "but that wouldn't be nearly as much fun."

"But the breaking up wasn't much fun either, was it?" asked Father Mick.

"What does walking a spiritual path tell us about the nature of relationships and how to make them work?" asked Robert.

"I've never been married," said Father Mick. "But I have counseled and listened to many married couples. The relationship that began with romance and lust often ends up as an exercise in fear and resentment. It's impossible to maintain the ecstatic high of their initial coupling. They lose their buzz. Because the relationship has no permanent basis, it collapses under its own weight."

"Sounds familiar," said Timmy.

Father Mick grinned. "Okay, but what if relationships could be made stable?"

"I'm not sure what you're driving at," said Timmy.

"The bond between a man and a woman will not be stable until it becomes grounded in the presence of God," said the priest.

"Do you really think God cares if Susie and I screw?" I asked.

"Oh, much more than that," said Father Mick. "If God's a participant in the relationship between two people, then every act of intimacy becomes a sacred event."

"Huh?" I blurted.

"Intimate sex between truly married people in the presence of God is perhaps the most spiritual act in which any two people can participate," said Father Mick, leaving us speechless. "You see," the priest said, "all relationships are sacred. We should never treat any relationship as anything less than holy."

"Great big yellow buttery balls of love!" said Robert.

"One more thing," Father Mick said, grinning. "Love, once born, never dies. Not divorce, not death, not anything in this world can break that bond. Here, let me read this." He opened the book on his lap and began to read. The book was The Prophet by Kahlil Gibran.

> *On Marriage*
>
> *You were born together, and together you shall be forever more.*
> *You shall be together when the white wings of death scatter your days.*
> *Ay, you shall be together even in the silent memory of God.*
> *But let there be spaces in your togetherness,*
> *And let the winds of the heavens dance between you.*
> *Love one another, but make not a bond of love:*
> *Let it rather be a moving sea between the shores of your souls.*

Fill each other's cup, but drink not from one cup.

Give one another of your bread, but eat not from the same loaf.

Sing and dance together and be joyous, but let each of you be alone,

Even as the strings of a lute are alone though they quiver with the same music.

Give your hearts, but not into each other's keeping.

For only the hand of Life can contain your hearts.

And stand together yet not too near together:

For the pillars of the temple stand apart,

And the oak tree and the cypress grow not in each other's shadow.

Re-people-ization

When Dr. Taylor was recovering from his alcoholism, there were no treatment centers which dealt with the problems that physicians face, so he went out and built one. At least once a week he liked to bend our ears with his personal take on recovery.

"An essential element of recovery is the process of re-people-ization." he said. "For years, as active alcoholics, we underwent progressive isolation from our coworkers and colleagues, from our friends and families, and finally from what remained of our Higher Power. To move forward with recovery, we must renew these old relationships. We can no longer live in isolation. We're social animals and require nourishing relationships with other humans in order to thrive."

Later Robert and I talked as we walked back to the apartments.

"I don't have to like anyone," he said, "but I must learn to love everyone."

"How the hell am I supposed to do that?" I asked.

"It's simple," said Robert. "We're all children of the same father, so we're all related in the largest possible sense. Since all relationships with a

Higher Power are by definition sacred then all relationships between human beings are also sacred. We need to learn to honor all, and I do mean all, of our relationships with other people. I think Jane said that."

"That's a lot to swallow," I said, thinking of the enemies I made when I was using.

"Look closely at every person you meet," said Robert. "Try to see below their outer appearance and actions. Look for the God within."

"Honor all relationships as sacred," I said, "because they are. Okay, but I'm not sure how successful I'll be."

Don't take the bait

Timmy and I were preparing dinner for tonight's AA meeting in our apartment. The menu was tuna casserole, green beans from a can, and frozen dinner rolls. Neither Timmy nor I were known for our culinary expertise.

Timmy was upset. He seemed to be having trouble opening the can of tuna fish. His face looked like a bowl of jello about to melt.

"My wife called," he blubbered. "She wants me to pay her back every cent of the cost of rehab. When we decided I should come here, we agreed to take the money out of savings. I don't know what to do. The bill here is over $12,000 already and I'm not done yet. Janet's really pissed. I feel like shit."

"How does she expect you to pay her back while you're in here?" I asked. "Do you have piles of money hidden someplace?"

"No, of course not. I have twenty bucks in my pocket," he moaned.

"And she knows this?" I asked.

"Of course, she does," he said.

"Maybe she's just trying to yank your chain?" I asked.

"She definitely knows how to punch my buttons," said Timmy.

"So, you're obsessing about something over which you have no control, and you've gotten yourself into a real snit," I said. "You swallowed the bait, hook, line, and sinker."

"I guess I did," said Timmy. "I never thought of it that way."

"If we don't take the hook," I said, "we avoid all this wringing of hands and gnashing of teeth. Or do you like it when she upsets you?"

"I do not!" said Timmy.

"To stop taking the hook, you have to recognize the bait for what it is," I said. "You no longer have to respond reflexively."

"Don't take the hook," said Timmy.

"And remember these words: God, grant me the serenity to accept the things I cannot change."

Low expectations, high serenity

Having finished our cups of non-caffeinated coffee, we assembled in a small classroom for Raphael's session.

"My expectations were always getting me in trouble," said Raphael. "If I expected a Mercedes-Benz for my birthday and instead I got a Porsche, I'd be crushed. It matters not that the Porsche cost more, was sexier, and came in midnight blue, it was not a Mercedes-Benz and therefore a disappointment. My expectations kept me from having any peace or satisfaction. If, on the other hand, I had kept my expectations low, then a 1976 Ford Pinto would have been quite satisfactory, and I would still have had my serenity. High expectations, low serenity. Low expectations, high serenity."

"Does that mean I should always expect nothing, then be satisfied with less?" asked Timmy.

"Who can answer Timmy's question?" asked Raphael.

"Absolutely not," said Mike, "but my expectations must be in line with reality. If my parents were gad-zillionaires, they might buy me a Porsche for my birthday. However, my parents are retired and live on a modest income, so I'm happy with a phone call, a birthday card, or a pair of hand-knitted socks."

"Good," said Raphael. "But let's make this a little more real. How about looking for a job? Willy?"

Wee Willy grinned his impish smile. "Whenever I applied for a job, I always expected to get hired on the spot as the new CEO and make $200,000 a year. But you know, I've applied for dozens of jobs and that's never happened."

Robert spoke up. "If I go to a job interview with outrageously high expectations, I'm bound to be disappointed. I'll do a lot better if my goal is to show up, fill out the application correctly, and present myself in the best light possible. That way I'm a success at every interview."

"Low expectations, high serenity. High expectations, low serenity," repeated Raphael. "There's a short prayer that touches on this idea, which I present for your consideration: God, let me love what I have."

Forgiveness

Father Mick took the podium for the morning spiritual and smiled benevolently at his flock of drunks and junkies.

"Forgiveness is all around me," said Father Mick, "but to obtain it, I must first forgive others. I've heard that prayers of forgiveness should be said only once for each person on your list. I guess my willingness hasn't been all it should be, because I generally have to pray several times to clear my resentments. Even today, old resentments and disappointments surface that require me to forgive someone. It's terribly important that I do so right away and not let the resentment fester." His kind gaze seemed to touch each face in the room.

"Consider this radical idea," he said. "If I wronged a shopkeeper by stealing a six-pack of beer, I can apologize for my wrong, pay him for the beer and make a commitment never to steal again. I've made amends for my behavior, but he cannot give me forgiveness. Forgiveness, I'm suggesting, is available only from my Higher Power. Contrary to what's written in many places, I believe that forgiveness is always there. I believe that at the moment of my quickening in the womb, I was granted forgiveness for every wrong I might possibly commit in my lifetime. Like the Prodigal Son, to claim my inheritance of forgiveness, all I have to do is ask!"

"I have to forgive myself as well. Otherwise, I'm stuck in the trap of spiritual pride, which says that my judgment is more important than God's."

"Lead me not into temptation," whispered Reggie.

Making amends

Timmy sat in Father Mick's study while Father Mick made coffee. Timmy's palms were sweaty, and he was sighing a lot. He was there to work on making amends. He held a list of his misdeeds in his hand.

"You know, you can't do this by yourself," said Father Mick.

"Eh?" Timmy looked up, rubbing his hands on his pants.

"You can't make amends by yourself. Too many people jump the gun and try to do it alone. Doesn't work. You'll need a sponsor to guide you."

"I'm worried I won't be able to do it at all," said Timmy. "I'm afraid to face some of those people."

"Don't worry, it's not as terrible as it sounds. Besides, what's the absolute worst that could happen? You get arrested, somebody throws a punch at you, or calls security to throw you out?"

"How do I begin?" asked Timmy. "How do I go about making amends for a lifetime of mistakes? Some people have died. Some moved away. Some won't even talk to me."

"Let's start with your moral inventory," said Father Mick. "Let me see what you've got there."

Looking as sheepish as only Timmy could, he handed the list to Father Mick.

"Remember, my son," said Father Mick, "your misdeeds are no worse than mine or anyone else's. Let's go over these one by one and see what we come up with."

In about an hours' time, they had divided Timmy's amends into three piles: those to do right away, those to do later time when conditions were right, and those that would probably never get done.

"After you get out of rehab and you have a permanent sponsor," said Father Mick, "go over this list with him, and with his guidance begin with the first group. Visit those people, either at home, or at the office, if necessary. Don't try to make friends or show them the error of their ways. Simply apologize for your part in whatever happened, then stop. Your job is to make amends. Simply apologizing isn't enough. You must change your behavior, permanently." He paused for a sip of coffee.

"You're there to remove the errors of the past from your heart, to lift the burden of the guilt you feel. How they respond is of no importance to you."

"What about my dad?" asked Timmy. "He's been dead ten years."

"Write him a letter just as if he were standing in front of you. Go to his grave and read the letter aloud. And remember, you can't ask for forgiveness for yourself until you've forgiven all those who've wronged you."

Later, Timmy shared his session with Reggie and me.

Reggie smiled. "I had to make amends to my ex-wife. We hadn't been on speaking terms for years, so I was more than a little hesitant to contact her. I called and said I wanted to make amends. To my surprise, she invited me over for coffee. We talked for a long time about my recovery and what

I was trying to do with my life. I must have struck a chord with her because she stretched her hand out to me.

"She said, Tell you what, I'll forgive you for everything you did to me, if you'll forgive me for everything I did to you".

"I didn't have to think twice about my answer. We shook hands and clinked our coffee cups. Now we often talk as co-parents and have dinner and holidays together with our children. Life is so much easier."

"My sponsor said that I needed to find a place in my heart that corresponds to the heart of the person I've wronged. I need to walk a mile in their shoes. I need to understand the effects of my mistakes on their lives and know the pain I caused. My actions had significant consequences that I must acknowledge."

Thinking more of others

Miguel had finished rehab five years ago and had been sober since. He was a friend of Bill's and we ran into him at the mall on Saturday afternoon. We invited him to share a cup of coffee and tell us about his new life.

"You've gone five years without drinking?" asked Timmy. "Don't you ever want to pick up a glass of wine or a bottle of beer?"

"Of course, I do," said Miguel, an obstetrician who had gone to medical school with Bill and was practicing in Atlanta. "After all, I'm an alcoholic. But just because it's in my nature to drink doesn't mean I have to. Today I have the tools to stay sober."

"Do you go to meetings every day?" asked Robert.

"In the first 365 days," he said, "I went to 432 meetings without missing a day. I go to fewer meetings now, but I pray and meditate every day. The key for me is the maintenance of my spiritual fitness."

"Did you have to give up your possessions?" asked Bill, the one with the new Jaguar.

"Actually," said Miguel, "in recovery I've been showered with more material blessings than ever before. But acquiring possessions is no longer what life is all about."

"Do you have fun?" asked Timmy, who was afraid that recovery would be like sitting in the front pew at church every day.

"I promised myself the first day I got sober," said Miguel, "that if recovery wasn't more fun than using, I'd go back to using. Right from the start, life became easier and more wonderful. I have lots of good times now. What's more, I can remember them."

We laughed at that.

"What's been the hardest thing you've encountered in your recovery?" I asked. "Making amends to other people?"

"Making amends proved a lot easier than I thought it would be," said Miguel. "My mother died in my second year, and that was difficult, but I didn't drink over it. Turning my will over to God was a problem at first but has gotten easier with each passing year."

"Most difficult by far has been learning to think more about others than myself. I'm basically self-centered and selfish and I'm certainly the center of my world. But I pray every day for God to make me a better person and to teach me to love my fellows as myself. Thinking of others first is a priority I aspire to, but have by no means achieved."

Helping others

The next day, after Jane's session, I headed toward the coffeepot and found myself behind Reggie. My friend was frowning. "What's up?" I asked.

Reggie sighed as he stirred his coffee.

"You remember when we talked about the great big yellow…"

"…buttery balls of love?" I asked. "How could I forget?"

"Well, I got a call from my friend Zack back in Memphis today," said

Reggie. He shook his head sadly. "Zack was Special Forces and came home with PTSD. He never could find his place back in the real world. Did a lot of drugs and booze, for all the good it did him."

"When I first met him, he had lost his two front teeth, his hair was scraggly halfway down his back, and he was eating nothing but raw food. He'd been denied disability, and he couldn't get along with his parents. I tried to help him see the goodness in himself."

"So you taught him the buttery balls of love thing?" I asked.

"Yeah," said Reggie, "He tried it on his parents, and it worked!"

"And?"

"Well, I hadn't heard from him in months, and like I said, he called today. His voice was unusually calm and peaceful. He's been diagnosed with a degenerative nervous condition. He's in a wheelchair and having trouble using his hands. He's selling everything he owns and moving into a nursing home."

Reggie paused.

"His doctor said he has less than six months to live. He's already having trouble breathing. I asked how he was taking all this. He said he was doing alright. Every time he falls into self-pity or starts getting depressed, he thinks about the great big yellow buttery balls of love and it makes him feel better. He was calling to thank me for that."

Reggie paused again.

"You always hope your words of kindness help someone, but you never know," he said, turning his face away.

"Now you know," I said.

Serenity

Timmy seemed lost in a cloud as we drove into the city for a fancy dinner out. There was a restaurant atop one of the skyscrapers that rotated a full 360 degrees while you ate, and we were all excited to experience it for ourselves. John, as usual, was driving.

"What's up Timmy?" asked Robert, putting his arm around the young pharmacist-gone-bad.

"I'm confused," said Timmy, starting to sound like me.

"About what?" asked Robert.

"About this serenity thing," he said. "What exactly is serenity? What is the serenity prayer all about? Help me out here, guys."

"Glad you asked," said Robert, eager to share. "Serenity, I've been told, is a state of mind."

My ears perked up. I was as eager as Timmy to hear what my mates had to say.

"True," said Reggie. "But it's more than that. It's one of those spiritual concepts that defy a rational definition. There are probably as many descriptions of serenity as there are people looking for it."

"Joy," said Robert, "it has to include joy. And peace."

"Being at peace with the world," said Mike, chewing on the end of his pen since we wouldn't let him smoke in the car. "Not struggling against all the crap I see in the world around me. Feeling at ease with life just the way it is."

Good luck with that, I thought.

"Not weighed down by the baggage and resentments of my past." said Reggie.

We will not regret the past nor wish to shut the door on it, I thought, remembering one of the AA promises.

"And not worrying about what may never happen," Reggie continued.

Robert recited a quote, as he was wont to do. "I am an old man and have known a great many troubles, but most of them never happened. Mark Twain said that."

I suddenly remembered a line from a Tom Petty song: Most things I worry 'bout, never happen anyway.

We let the valet park the car and looked up at the glass elevator that stretched to the top floor. The elevator was on the outside, so you could see the city as you scaled the heights of the tallest building in Atlanta.

"Father Mick talks about living in the moment," said Mike as we inched our way upward.

Robert produced another quote: "Don't dwell in the past, don't dream of the future, concentrate on the present moment. Peace comes from within. Don't seek it without. The Buddha said that."

Mike went on. "Father Mick said, when I'm living in the moment, my mind is still, quiet. I'm filled with the peace and joy of the universe. He says that God lives in the moment."

"Heavy," said Tommy, catching his breath as he looked down from the heights.

I recalled Father Mick's session from a few days before.

"I'm a big fan of Thomas Jefferson," he said. "In the Declaration of Independence, Jefferson suggested that we're guaranteed the right to life, liberty, and the pursuit of happiness. He knew that in this life we are not promised happiness. Whenever I reached out for happiness it always seemed to vanish like the pot of gold at the end of the rainbow."

"In our old world, we looked for happiness everywhere: a promotion at work, a hot new girlfriend, or a fast, shiny new car. I got high in my anticipation. But if these things got me high, my buzz always faded rapidly. What I was told, and what I have had glimpses of, is that when I find serenity, happiness follows, tagging along like a puppy dog, bright-eyed and grinning. Happiness is the child of serenity. To find happiness, first find serenity.."

"How long will it take to find *my* serenity?" Timmy asked. I still have times when my head's filled with jumbled-up thoughts. I've been working hard on the Steps but I'm not happy, joyous, or free."

"A year," said Father Mick. "For most people, it takes a year to find any significant degree of serenity."

I was appropriately discouraged.

The good father continued, "I'd been out of rehab for about four months when one summer morning I awoke with a strange feeling of happiness with no idea why. I could hear a mockingbird singing outside my window. Nothing was bothering me. I had nothing I had to jump up and do. There was no sense of time. I didn't feel old or young. There was only the moment I was in and nothing else. You might say I was centered. This was peace. It only lasted the morning, then it was gone."

I suddenly remembered the same feeling not too many days ago. For a few hours, and a few hours only, I was at peace.

"Over the last few years, my serenity has come and gone, each time longer and deeper than the time before," said Father Mick. "I can remember the ecstasy of two full months of peace, which collapsed into a time of turmoil only to resurface some months later. Then I found myself in a six-month period of bliss, but it faded as well. In time, my periods of peace have come more often and lasted longer. Now, bad days are getting further and further apart."

"When you found this peace," asked Reggie, "where were you, I mean, spiritually?"

"First," said Father Mick, "acceptance was always there. I've had clinical depression since my university days and at times my depression has been severe. When I've had peace, I've also been at peace with my mental illness."

"My serenity seems related to how much of my ego I can surrender to my Higher Power. This is what 'Let go and let God' is all about. There seems to be an inverse relationship between the level of my self-will, and the level of my ability to lean back into the flow of the spirit. The lower my ego, the more serenity I can let in. With time, I've gotten better at this process, but I'm so hard-headed and stubborn that progress has been slow. Still, I persist."

We completed a full circle by the time we finished our meal, gazing at the beauty of the city below. For dessert, we had a large helping of contentment.

"Tell me about the serenity prayer?" asked Timmy, sipping his latte.

"God grant me the serenity to accept the things I cannot change, the courage to change the things I can, and the wisdom to know the difference," recited Robert. "Reinhold Niebuhr."

"It's one of the spiritual tools in the kit of my recovery," said Reggie. "Each morning when I get up, I have a list of items, issues, and situations that need my attention. The list is always too long and too difficult for me to tackle by myself. The prayer tells me to separate those items that are my work from those that I must leave for God. Now comes the wisdom part, where I know which things go in my pile, and which things I have no control over. These go in God's pile. Oftentimes, I need a measure of serenity to accept that these items are beyond my control. To complete my list will often require a bit of courage, you know, doing the next right thing, even if you're afraid."

Robert was at it again. "We will suddenly realize that God is doing for us what we could not do for ourselves. The prayer isn't just a spiritual ideal but a practical tool for everyday life."

For some reason, going down in the elevator, physically suspended twenty floors above the ground, was infinitely frightening. With one hand I held on to Mike, the other hand clutching the side rail.

"I feel like I'm falling," I gasped.

"Me, too," whispered Mike, holding on to me.

A New Way of Living

By sharing the truths we have found, we can
be of benefit to others.

Judge not.

Belief in dualities only leads to judgment,
resentments, and suffering.

There is only God and his world.

All spiritual principles boil down to one:
I should treat others the way I want to be treated.

When I send the blessings of the Universe out
to those around me, I necessarily secure those
blessings for myself.

Maintenance of my integrity, my spiritual
fitness, is required for my sobriety.

If I am to be happy, I must first accept the
world as it is, not as I want it to be.

I can change nothing in the world.
I can only change my way of looking at the world.

The Fine Points

"There are only two mistakes one can make along the road to truth;
Not going all the way, and not starting."
—The Buddha

Grace and fellowship

Leon was discharged from rehab and sent home with a good report. He called me a week later.

"Still sober?" he asked me.

"Yes, and you?"

"Got another AA chip," said Leon. "A woman at the meeting picked up a one-year chip at the same time. She said something that stuck with me. Someone asked how she had done it, stayed sober for a whole year."

"What did she say?" I asked, already knowing the answer.

"She said she couldn't do it, at least not by herself." Leon smiled into the phone. "She said, it's by the grace of God and the fellowship of these rooms I haven't found it necessary to drug or drink in over a year."

"No one can do it alone," I said. "If we could, we wouldn't have to go to rehab."

Parting words

Raphael was in a particularly effusive mood. He had been walking in the gardens after lunch and he was filled with the happiness of a peaceful man. He almost bubbled as he began our afternoon session.

"Don't drink! Go to meetings! Have fun!" said Raphael as if leading a pep rally cheer. "Having fun is an essential part of life. But no real joy is possible if I don't stay sober and keep spiritually fit."

"What else?" asked an eager Timmy.

"Who knows what H-A-L-T means?" asked Raphael.

Mike answered. "Hungry, angry, lonely, tired. Don't get too hungry, too angry, too lonely, or too tired."

"Why not?" asked Raphael.

"Because my thinking gets disordered and I make mistakes," said Reggie.

"When most of you arrived here," Raphael continued, "you probably felt like you were giving up the best parts of your old life. How many feel that way now?"

A few hands went up in the room, but only from the newcomers.

"I've given up nothing worth keeping," Mike said slowly, "but if you'd told me that when I got here, I wouldn't have believed you."

"I'm giving up hangovers, blackouts, and trying to control the world," said Robert, "and today, when I wake up, I know where my shoes are."

"If I give up my affair," said Timmy, "maybe my wife will take me back. I'd like that."

"I'm giving up the tracks in my arm," I said, "and having to wear long sleeves in the summer to hide them."

"I can enjoy myself without worrying about getting caught," said Robert.

"You can live your lives without having to wear a mask," said Raphael. "One last and very important item, the more people I have looking after my disease, the better off I am. It would not be unreasonable to have an addictionologist, a psychiatrist, a sponsor, and a psychologist all participating in your care. As Dr. Taylor says, the more people I'm accountable to, the better off I am."

"Kinda sounds like the old Greek thing," said Timmy. "You know, a sound mind in a sound body."

"Except your mind makes a sound as awful as your guitar playing," said Robert.

Raspberries followed.

"One last thing," said Raphael. "Pray and meditate every day—and I mean that."

In the moment

A few days later, Mike and I were hanging out in front of the center. The late afternoon sun gilded the young maples that dotted the parking lot. Unexpectedly, the world around me changed abruptly. Suddenly, the trees popped out of the landscape, like opening a child's pop-up book. The colors of the leaves glowed like I had never seen them before. The grass under my feet shimmered in iridescent green. I looked at Mike and he looked back at me with his shit-eating grin.

We were sharing the same experience. The landscape had gone from a flat 2-D background to a vivid 3-D world. In this moment, I was content and comfortable in my own skin. My mind was clear of all distractions and free of worry. I didn't dare speak, lest the spell be broken. I was living in the moment. I had found serenity.

"Now I understand why we're doing all this work," I said. "Now it all makes sense."

"When I went through rehab before," said Mike, "I never experienced this. Whatever just happened, I want more of it. Maybe I can make it this time."

"Mike," I said softly, "why do you think you relapsed?"

"I thought I had this thing licked," he said. "I quit going to meetings and started visiting the ladies in the strip clubs. I quit doing my morning meditation. I was stupid."

"You are definitely not stupid," I said. "Maybe we'll both make it."

Summing up

In celebration of the departure of Robert and Mike, we met for dinner with Father Mick at a local sushi bar. Timmy and Reggie completed the table.

"I've never had sushi before," said Father Mick. "I'm not too sure about eating raw fish."

"Back home, we call it bait," said Reggie. "You put it on the end of a hook and throw it in the river."

"Don't be afraid," said Mike. "I've had sushi lots of times and I've never gotten sick."

"The green stuff gives the fish more flavor," I said to Father Mick, tongue in cheek. "It's called Wasabi. You'll want to put on a lot."

The waiter served the first round of rice and raw fish. Father Mick slathered wasabi on his and took a huge bite. In seconds, his face turned red as he frantically reached for his water glass. he rest of us tried to avoid laughing but with only limited success. When the steam cleared from his ears, Father Mick spoke.

"My," he said, "that was *really* good. I think I'll have some more."

"Try the ginger this time," I suggested. "You'll like it."

Father Mick ate the ginger-soaked tuna roll and grinned.

"I've always been a big fan of firehouse Mexican chili," he said. I'm really enjoying myself. I guess there was nothing to be afraid of after all—which sounds like a good topic for my final sermon for you two." He looked at Robert and Mike.

Having finished the first round of food, we settled back to listen.

"Someone in seminary told me the words fear and faith are connected more than three hundred times in the Bible."

"Seems like it might be important, then," said Timmy.

"Faith is what replaces fear," said Reggie. "Fear not, O ye of little faith."

"Exactly," said Father Mick. "The goal is to live a life that is free of fear."

"Love is the opposite of fear, right?" asked Timmy.

"Right," said Mike, "and it's fear that brings out my character defects. By dealing with my fears, I reduce my faults."

"I know that fear has driven my life and that it pushes me to make wrong choices," said Reggie.

"Fear makes me wear a mask to hide my true self," I said.

"As children of God," said Father Mick, "our inheritance is a life that's happy, joyous, and free of fear, a life based on love."

"God is love," said Timmy.

Father Mick nodded and grinned at Timmy.

"My innocent one," he said, "you give me such joy." He looked around the table with his most loving smile.

"Fear is the great paralyzer," he said, "and perhaps the major cause of failing to stay sober. Every time I use prayer to defeat fear, I grow inside, and that growth is never lost."

"A life lived in love, and free of fear," said Timmy.

The waiter brought the next round, California rolls and eel. By this time, we were all eager for the raw fish.

"I was afraid this stuff would be really bad," said Reggie, "but I have to admit, I like it!"

"Isn't that condemnation prior to investigation?" asked Mike.

"Yes," said Robert, judging is bad for my emotional health."

"The other way to say that," said Father Mick, "is that I must learn to accept the world as it is. Remember, that's our new definition of perfection. God's world is perfect just the way it is. I only need the eyes to see it."

"Matt said if I judge God's handiwork," said Timmy, "then I'm judging God, which is something I should avoid."

"The more I judge others—any person, place, or thing—the further I am from my serenity," said Robert.

"If you think about it," said Reggie, "I can't judge the path another person is on, because I have no way of knowing what's in their mind or their heart."

"I won't try to set standards for the behavior of those around me," said Robert. "Especially when the standards I set are impossible for even me to reach."

"Judging others comes from my inferiority complex," said Father Mick. "A good first step in removing this shortcoming is to show tolerance for others. But the largest hurdle may be the requirement that I forgive everyone for everything."

"Limitations," said Mike. "When I judge someone, I necessarily put limitations on them, and I've learned that I shouldn't limit myself, my recovery, or my Higher Power."

"If I want to live a life free of fear and find the serenity that's my inheritance," said Robert, "then I'll have to learn to love everyone I come in contact with."

"But what about those SOBs who think they're better than me?" asked Timmy.

Father Mick just sighed. "Leave them alone and they'll do just fine. Could you pass me the wasabi?"

The day of Mike's leave-taking had finally arrived. Robert had gone the day before. I hated to see my friend Mike go, but I was happy for him.

"When will you start back to work?" I asked. We walked toward the parking lot where Mike's car was packed and ready to go.

"I have a week off, then I work half time for a month before I hit the grind full time," he said. "And you?"

"I wish I had a good answer. If I went back to medicine now, I think it would kill me."

"I remember you saying that the way you practiced medicine fed into your addiction."

"Yeah, it's going to take a while for some of my scars to heal. That's all I know for sure."

Mike stopped and turned toward me. "You know if you get into trouble, or start Jones-ing really bad, you can always call me."

"Yeah, I know. And that goes likewise, I'm sure."

He looked into my eyes. "What's the problem?" he asked.

"The problem is addiction," I replied, beginning the catechism.

"And what's the answer?" he asked.

"The answer is recovery," I answered.

"And how shall we live now?"

"We shall live happy, joyous and free—free from fear."

I put my arms around him and gave him a hug. In less than a minute he was in his little green sports car, around the corner, out of sight, and on his way back to New Jersey.

As I headed back toward the apartment, I realized that my path would be much longer than the highway to Newark. Ahead of me were the Beast, the Angel, and the Madman, all vying for control of my life. No matter how long or soberly I lived, the Beast would always lurk somewhere close, ready to return at the first slip. The Madman was woven into the fabric of my thinking—an insanity so insidious that some days I could not tell his thoughts from my own. But my Angel, my saving grace, would always be near, pointing the way home.

The Fine Points

Living in the moment,

without the weight of the past

pulling me down,

without fear of the future,

unburdened by negativity,

living beyond fear and resentments,

is the goal and the reward of recovery.

ANNOTATED BIBLIOGRAPHY

Alcoholics Anonymous: The Story of How Many Thousands of Men and Women Have Recovered from Alcoholism. Fourth Edition. Alcoholics Anonymous World Services, New York, NY, 2001. First published in 1939 and known as The Big Book, its lessons are as valid as ever. My copy is underlined in a hundred places. The Big Book was my manual for early recovery and it continues to provide a source of spiritual wisdom. It is available at most AA meeting houses, on Amazon.com, and online.

Twelve Steps and Twelve Traditions, Alcoholics Anonymous. Alcoholics Anonymous World Services, New York, NY, 1952. Written as an expansion of the ideas presented in The Big Book. A Bill of Rights for AA.

Bibliography

The Sermon on the Mount: The Key to Success in Life, by Emmet Fox. HarperOne, San Francisco, 1934. If a book can save a person's life, then this book saved mine. Not only does Mr. Fox reexamine the Sermon on the Mount as it appears in the Book of Matthew, he provides a key to an understanding of spirituality. He opened my eyes to a new way of looking at the world and at my life. In the days before the Big Book was written, AA mythology says this book was the manual for newcomers.

The Essential Rumi, New Expanded Edition, by Jalal al-Din Rumi, translated by Coleman Barks and John Moyne. HarperOne, San Francisco, 2004. Rumi was the first of the Sufi masters, and he took his spiritual truth from all the religious traditions of his time. His poetry touches on the deepest issues of human spirituality. Coleman Barks' translations are wonderful. Meditation, recovery, poetry, and spirituality all in one! My favorite small volume of Rumi is **Birdsong: Fifty-Three Short Poems**, Maypop, Athens, GA, 1993.

The Prophet, by Kahlil Gibran. Alfred A. Knopf, New York, 1973. Enough spiritual wisdom is packed in these few pages to last a lifetime.

Self-Esteem: The New Reformation, by Robert H. Schuller. W Publishing Group (Thomas Nelson), Nashville, TN, 1982. Long-time pastor of the Crystal Cathedral Ministries, Rev. Schuller preached the concepts of spiritual recovery under the guise of Christianity. My Jewish friend Mike called me one day and said, Hey man, you gotta listen to this guy. He preaches recovery.

The Holy Bible. I have come to think of the Bible as a manual for the development of the soul and Jesus as the supreme spiritual master of mankind. My edition is always open to the Book of Matthew. I prefer the **King James Version,** the one with the large print. The more modern translations-for-today versions not only lack the power and poetry of KJV but often lose the meaning altogether.

The Bhagavad Gita, translated by Juan Mascaro. Penguin Books, London, 1962. My first sponsor was an African-American ex-heroin addict and a practicing Hindu. He taught me to chant Hare Krishna and introduced me to the Gita. I don't chant anymore, but the wisdom I found in this 2,500-year-old inspired work is as relevant and necessary as that of the Bible. Mr. Mascaro's translation is the classic one and, for my money, the most powerful and direct. A related and useful translation is **Bhagavad Gītā as It Is,** a translation of the Bhagavad Gita, with commentary, by A. C. Bhaktivedanta Swami Prabhupada, founder of the International Society for Krishna Consciousness. He expounds and explains the Gita in detail from an entirely different point of view.

The Dhammapada, translated by Eknath Easwaran, Nilgiri Press, Tomales, CA. 2007. Like Jesus and Socrates, The Buddha never wrote anything down. But his followers later recorded a series of lessons used for his students. As I read the text, I underlined what to me seemed to be important passages. When I reread my underlining, I found that each would have made a good topic for an AA meeting. Easwaran also translated a wonderful version of the **Bhagavad Gītā** as well (Shambala Library, Boston, 2004).

Wherever You Go, There You Are, Mindfulness, Meditation In Everyday Life, by Jon Kabat-Zinn, Hyperion, New, 1994. A follow-up of his earlier book, **Full Catastrophe Living,** which describes how to use the concept of mindfulness in times of emotional or physical stress, this volume is a guidebook to using meditation and mindfulness.

Touchstones: A Book Of Daily Meditations For Men. A collection by various authors. Hazelden Foundation, Center City, MN, 1986. Hazelden has published a host of fine books dealing with nearly every aspect of addiction and recovery. Touchstones is not just for men anymore. For years, this book provided me with a short bit of necessary inspiration every morning for living in a seemingly insane world.

Meditations with Meister Eckhart, by Matthew Fox. Bear & Company, Rochester, Vermont, 1983. Eckhart was a German theologian in the 13th century. Today, he is known as a mystic. His words, cast here as meditations, are clean, pure, and simple. An excellent way to start the day.

The Science of Mind, by Ernest Holmes. Dodd, Mead and Company, New York, 1938. Mr. Holmes takes the ideas championed by Mr. Fox, that the outer world is but the outpouring of the thoughts in my mind. He carries this idea to its logical extreme.

Celebration of Discipline: The Path to Spiritual Growth, by Richard J. Foster. Harper San Francisco, San Francisco, 1988. A Christian apologist, Mr. Foster offers a series of useful disciplines, including meditation, prayer, fasting, simplicity, solitude, celebration and more. Good stuff from within the established Protestant Church.

The Seven Spiritual Laws of Success: A Practical Guide to the Fulfillment of Your Dreams, by Deepak Chopra. New World Library/Amber-Allen Publishing, San Francisco, 1994. My first psychiatrist gave me this book. Coming from a background of Hinduism and medicine, Dr. Chopra describes a set of spiritual principles. He has written many other excellent books.

Conversations with God: An Uncommon Dialogue, Books 1-3, by Neale Donald Walsch. G. P. Putnam›s Sons, New York, NY, 1996. Mr. Walsch picked up a yellow pad and began to write. When he was done, he had written three books detailing his conversations with God. Informing knowledge from unconventional sources.

The Dragon Doesn't Live Here Anymore, by Allen Cohan. Ballantine Books, New York, NY, 1993. Mr. Cohen synthesizes spiritual wisdom from a multitude of sources, yielding a work filled with insights and especially relevant to the recovering alcoholic and addict.

Remember, Be Here Now, by Ram Dass (Richard Alpert). The Lama Foundation, Questa, NM, 1971. Mr. Alpert was a professor at Harvard down the hall from Timothy Leary. Leary took LSD; Alpert went to India. When Alpert returned, he wrote his now-famous book on what he learned there: that living in the moment is everything.

Codependent No More & Beyond Codependency, by Melody Beattie. Mjf Books (Fine Creative Media, Inc.), New York, NY, 2001. Ms. Beattie is the first and last word on codependency, especially as it relates to addiction. Required reading.

The Shack, by Wm. Paul Young. Windblown Media, Los Angeles, 2007. More learning from unconventional sources. An allegory about God, the universe, and me.

www.ingramcontent.com/pod-product-compliance
Lightning Source LLC
LaVergne TN
LVHW091534060526
838200LV00036B/605